every young man's battle guide

Weapons for the War
Against Sexual Temptation

every young man's battle guide

Stephen Arterburn
Fred Stoeker with Mike Yorkey

WATERBROOK
P R E S S

EVERY YOUNG MAN'S BATTLE GUIDE
PUBLISHED BY WATERBROOK PRESS
2375 Telstar Drive, Suite 160
Colorado Springs, Colorado 80920
A division of Random House, Inc.

ISBN 1-57856-737-8

Copyright © 2003 by Stephen Arterburn, Fred Stoeker, and Mike Yorkey

Published in association with the literary agency of Alive Communications, Inc., 7680 Goddard
Street, Suite 200, Colorado Springs, CO 80920.

Printed in China
2003—First Edition

10 9 8 7 6 5 4 3 2 1

contents

introduction

You'd have to be living in a cave in Outer Mongolia not to notice how everybody is talking about sex these days. It seems to be the focal point of practically every conversation. Unfortunately, those with the loudest voices hail from Hollywood.

Many of the male characters in today's movies and television shows are depicted as horny guys with stunted personalities, traveling through life with nothing more on their minds than girls—and getting some sexual action. The writers of these sexually charged films and sitcoms build their plots around a simple yet familiar formula: Boy meets Girl, Boy chases Girl, Boy gets Girl in bed, Boy and Girl have lots of fun. Boy and Girl experience no guilt and no consequences as they ride off into the sunset in their azure blue BMW M3 ragtop. Roll the credits.

But in the real word, sex is never quite as simple as the media would have us believe. Hollywood producers love showing us the night of passion, but they conveniently bypass the reality of the morning after: the feelings of remorse, the girl waking up to realize she was nothing more than a convenient object for fulfilling a guy's sexual desire, the visit to a doctor's office because a former sexual partner said it would be a good idea to get checked, or the ominous phone message from a girlfriend who thinks she's pregnant.

So why is the portrayal of sex so far from reality? The fact is,

Hollywood—and our sex-crazed culture—has turned its back on God's advice and tried to reverse centuries of biblical principles. According to Hollywood's credo, being good (like staying out of bed before marriage) is actually bad for you, but being bad (as in indulging in frequent premarital sex) is actually good for you.

Our Creator knew this would happen. Several centuries ago the prophet Isaiah quoted God as saying, "Destruction is certain for those who say that evil is good and good is evil; that dark is light and light is dark; that bitter is sweet and sweet is bitter" (Isaiah 5:20, NLT).

Maybe you've begun to question the truth of the messages you've been hearing. Maybe you suspect that sex is a bit more complicated and dangerous than you realized—either because of personal experience or seeing the impact on your friends. The fact that you are holding this book means that you are at least willing to hear what God has to say about sex, and that's good news, because He sure has a lot to say. He has given us clear direction on everything from how we should treat the opposite sex to how and why we should abstain from sexual activity until marriage.

Keep in mind, though, that God is not some big killjoy in the sky, wanting to put a damper on your attempts at fun. First and foremost, His words are those of a loving Creator who wants to spare His children—you *and* her—the agony that sexual sin can bring. He wants to spare us the emotional pain of the morning after and the physical distress from sexually transmitted diseases that inevitably arise from promiscuous sexual encounters—or that seven-pound "surprise" nine months later. God only wants the best for us, a better future that includes "plans to prosper you and not to harm you, plans to give you hope," as His Word states in Jeremiah 29:11 (NIV).

As you will read in the following pages, the Lord of the universe delivers some straight talk about sex that goes against what you've been hearing. God doesn't go for that if-it-feels-good-do-it stuff, nor does He let us make up our minds based on which way today's cultural winds happen to be blowing. Instead, God's standard for sexual purity can be captured in a single Bible verse: "But among you there must not be even a hint of sexual immorality, or of any kind of impurity" (Ephesians 5:3, NIV).

For young single guys, that verse may prompt some challenging questions. What does a "hint" mean? How far can you go with a girl when you're alone? How far can you go with yourself when you're alone?

These are great questions, and you'll receive some straight answers in *Every Young Man's Battle Guide*.

God's owner's manual
regarding sexual conduct

Let's go to the source and check out what the Bible has to say on the subject of sexual conduct. Did you know that in nearly every book of the New Testament we're commanded to avoid sexual impurity? Here's a selection of passages that teach God's concern for our sexual purity.

—*adapted from* **Every Young Man's Battle**

GOD'S DEFINITION OF SEXUAL PURITY

Amber is a twenty-year-old single woman attending a Christian college. "I wish I would have been told more specifically what 'sexual purity' really meant when I was growing up in the church," she said. "I was always taught that sexual purity meant 'no sexual intercourse,' but then I read and loved the definition given in *Every Man's Battle:* 'Sexual purity is receiving no sexual gratification from anything or anyone outside of your husband or wife.' That's a black-and-white definition that young people need to be taught. If you don't do anything else, please stress this definition."

—*adapted from* **Every Young Man's Battle**

It is God's will that you should be sanctified: that you should avoid sexual immorality; that each of you should learn to control his own body in a way that is holy and honorable, not in passionate lust like the heathen, who do not know God.

1 THESSALONIANS 4:3-5, NIV

But immorality or any impurity or greed must not even be named among you, as is proper among saints.

EPHESIANS 5:3, NASB

Away then with sinful, earthly things; deaden the evil desires lurking within you; have nothing to do with sexual sin, impurity, lust and shameful desires; don't worship the good things of life, for that is idolatry.

COLOSSIANS 3:5, TLB

And that means killing off everything connected with that way of death: sexual promiscuity, impurity, lust, doing whatever you feel like whenever you feel like it, and grabbing whatever attracts your fancy. That's a life shaped by things and feelings instead of by God.

COLOSSIANS 3:5, MSG

What I meant was that you are not to keep company with anyone who claims to be a…Christian but indulges in sexual sins…. Don't even eat lunch with such a person.

1 CORINTHIANS 5:11, TLB

RUN—DON'T WALK—AWAY FROM SEXUAL IMMORALITY

I appeal to you therefore, brethren, by the mercies of God, to present your bodies as a living sacrifice, holy and acceptable to God, which is your spiritual worship. Do not be conformed to this world but be transformed by the renewal of your mind, that you may prove what is the will of God, what is good and acceptable and perfect.

ROMANS 12:1-2, RSV

Run away from sexual sin! No other sin so clearly affects the body as this one does. For sexual immorality is a sin against your own body.

1 CORINTHIANS 6:18, NLT

For if you are living according to the flesh, you must die; but if by the Spirit you are putting to death the deeds of the body, you will live.

ROMANS 8:13, NASB

Finally, brethren, whatever is true, whatever is honorable, whatever is just, whatever is pure, whatever is lovely, whatever is gracious, if there is any excellence, if there is anything worthy of praise, think about these things. What you have learned and received and heard and seen in me, do; and the God of peace will be with you.

PHILIPPIANS 4:8-9, RSV

But if you give yourself to the Lord, you and Christ are joined together as one person.

That is why I say to run from sex sin. No other sin affects the body as this one does. When you sin this sin it is against your own body.

1 Corinthians 6:17-18, tlb

As for the Gentile Christians, all we ask of them is what we already told them in a letter: …they should stay away from all sexual immorality.

Acts 21:25, nlt

Abstain…from sexual immorality.

Acts 15:20, niv

Beloved, I implore you as aliens and strangers and exiles [in this world] to abstain from the sensual urges (the evil desires, the passions of the flesh, your lower nature) that wage war against the soul. [Live] as free people, [yet] without employing your freedom as a pretext for wickedness; but [live at all times] as servants of God.

1 Peter 2:11,16, amp

You are to abstain from…sexual immorality.

Acts 15:29, niv

See that no one is sexually immoral.

Hebrews 12:16, niv

WHAT THE BIBLE HAS TO SAY ABOUT HOMOSEXUALITY

Do not practice homosexuality; it is a detestable sin.

LEVITICUS 18:22, NLT

Don't you know that those who do wrong will have no
share in the Kingdom of God? Don't fool yourselves.
Those who indulge in sexual sin, who are idol worshipers,
adulterers, male prostitutes, homosexuals…none of these
will have a share in the Kingdom of God.

1 CORINTHIANS 6:9-10, NLT

In the same way the men also abandoned natural relations with women and were inflamed with lust for one
another. Men committed indecent acts with other men, and
received in themselves the due penalty for their perversion.

ROMANS 1:27, NIV

WHAT JESUS SAID ABOUT LUST

But don't think you've preserved your virtue simply by
staying out of bed. Your heart can be corrupted by lust
even quicker than your body. Those leering looks you
think nobody notices—they also corrupt. Let's not pretend
this is easier than it really is. If you want to live a morally
pure life, here's what you have to do: You have to blind
your right eye the moment you catch it in a lustful leer.

You have to choose to live one-eyed or else be dumped on a moral trash pile.

MATTHEW 5:28-29, MSG

EXAMINE YOUR THOUGHT LIFE FREQUENTLY

Turn your back on the turbulent desires of youth and give your positive attention to goodness, integrity, love, and peace.

TIMOTHY 2:22, PHILLIPS

Don't allow love to turn into lust, setting off a downhill slide into sexual promiscuity, filthy practices, or bullying greed.

EPHESIANS 5:3, MSG

Remember all the commands of the LORD, that you may obey them and not prostitute yourselves by going after the lusts of your own hearts and eyes.

NUMBERS 15:39, NIV

Lust not after her beauty in thine heart; neither let her take thee with her eyelids.

PROVERBS 6:25, KJV

You have heard that the law of Moses says, "Do not commit adultery." But I say, anyone who even looks at a woman with lust in his eye has already committed adultery with her in his heart. So if your eye—even if it is your good eye—causes you to lust, gouge it out and throw it away. It is better for you to lose one part of your body than for your whole body to be thrown into hell. And if your hand—even if it is your stronger hand—causes you to sin, cut it off and throw it away. It is better for you to lose one part of your body than for your whole body to be thrown into hell.

MATTHEW 5:27-30, NLT

For God has not called us to be dirty-minded and full of lust, but to be holy and clean. If anyone refuses to live by these rules he is not disobeying the rules of men but of God who gives his Holy Spirit to you.

1 THESSALONIANS 4:7-8, TLB

For they mouth empty, boastful words and, by appealing to the lustful desires of sinful human nature, they entice people who are just escaping from those who live in error.

2 PETER 2:18, NIV

But a man must examine himself, and in so doing he is to eat of the bread and drink of the cup. For he who eats and drinks, eats and drinks judgment to himself if he does not judge the body rightly. For this reason many among you are weak and sick, and a number sleep. But if we judged ourselves rightly, we would not be judged. But when we are judged, we are disciplined by the Lord so that we will not be condemned along with the world.

1 CORINTHIANS 11:28-32, NASB

For all that is in the world—the lust of the flesh, the lust of the eyes, and the pride of life—is not of the Father but is of the world.

1 JOHN 2:16, NKJV

TODAY'S CHOICES WILL AFFECT YOU TOMORROW

Let's say you do something stupid, like stick your hand into a fire. If you leave your hand in the flames long enough, you'll feel the immediate consequences of excruciating pain. An even dumber action, however, would be to think that you're different and stronger than everyone else, believing you can put your hand in a campfire and not be burned. Since everyone knows that fire's consequences are instantaneous, few men play with fire.

Sin has a different timetable, however. You might sin for years and never experience the consequences, but they will come.

—Every Young Man's Battle

That is why God let go of them and let them do all these evil things, so that even their women turned against God's natural plan for them and indulged in sex sin with each other. And the men, instead of having a normal sex relationship with women, burned with lust for each other, men doing shameful things with other men and, as a result, getting paid within their own souls with the penalty they so richly deserved.

ROMANS 1:26-28, TLB

They don't care anymore about right and wrong and have given themselves over to impure ways. They stop at nothing, being driven by their evil minds and reckless lusts.

EPHESIANS 4:19, TLB

For out of the heart come evil thoughts, murder, adultery, sexual immorality, theft, false testimony, slander.

MATTHEW 15:19, NIV

Stop acting so proud and haughty!
    Don't speak with such arrogance!
The LORD is a God who knows your deeds;
    and he will judge you for what you have done.

1 SAMUEL 2:3, NLT

Even a child is known by his deeds,
Whether what he does is pure and right.

PROVERBS 20:11, NKJV

I said to myself, "In due season God will judge everything man does, both good and bad."

ECCLESIASTES 3:17, TLB

I am afraid that when I come again my God may humiliate me before you, and I may mourn over many of those who have sinned in the past and not repented of the impurity, immorality and sensuality which they have practiced.

2 CORINTHIANS 12:21, NASB

You can be sure that no immoral, impure, or greedy person will inherit the Kingdom of Christ and of God. For a greedy person is really an idolater who worships the things of this world.

EPHESIANS 5:5, NLT

What comes out of a man is what makes him "unclean." For from within, out of men's hearts, come evil thoughts, sexual immorality, theft, murder, [and] adultery.

MARK 7:20-21, NIV

When you follow the desires of your sinful nature, your lives will produce these evil results: sexual immorality, impure thoughts, eagerness for lustful pleasure, idolatry, participation in demonic activities, hostility, quarreling, jealousy, outbursts of anger, selfish ambition, divisions, the feeling that everyone is wrong except those in your own little group, envy, drunkenness, wild parties, and other kinds of sin. Let me tell you again, as I have before, that anyone living that sort of life will not inherit the Kingdom of God.

GALATIANS 5:19-21, NLT

So put to death the sinful, earthly things lurking within you. Have nothing to do with sexual sin, impurity, lust, and shameful desires. Don't be greedy for the good things of this life, for that is idolatry. God's terrible anger will come upon those who do such things.

COLOSSIANS 3:5-6, NLT

Don't you know that those who do wrong will have no share in the Kingdom of God? Don't fool yourselves. Those who indulge in sexual sin, who are idol worshipers, adulterers, male prostitutes, homosexuals, thieves, greedy people, drunkards, abusers, and swindlers—none of these will have a share in the Kingdom of God.… But our bodies were not made for sexual immorality. They were made for the Lord, and the Lord cares about our bodies.… Run away from sexual sin!

1 CORINTHIANS 6:9-10,13,18, NLT

There's more to sex than mere skin on skin. Sex is as much spiritual mystery as physical fact. As written in Scripture,

"The two become one." Since we want to become spiritually one with the Master, we must not pursue the kind of sex that avoids commitment and intimacy, leaving us more lonely than ever—the kind of sex that can never "become one."

1 CORINTHIANS 6:16, MSG

WHAT GOD DESIRES FOR YOU

For God wants you to be holy and pure, and to keep clear of all sexual sin so that each of you will marry in holiness and honor—not in lustful passion as the heathen do, in their ignorance of God and his ways.... For God has not called us to be dirty-minded and full of lust, but to be holy and clean.

1 THESSALONIANS 4:3-5,7, TLB

But you are not in darkness, brethren, for that day to surprise you like a thief. For you are all sons of light and sons of the day; we are not of the night or of darkness. So then let us not sleep, as others do, but let us keep awake and be sober. For those who sleep sleep at night, and those who get drunk are drunk at night. But, since we belong to the day, let us be sober, and put on the breastplate of faith and love, and for a helmet the hope of salvation.

1 THESSALONIANS 5:4-8, RSV

Evil plans are an abomination to the LORD,
But pleasant words are pure.

PROVERBS 15:26, NASB

The LORD hates people with twisted hearts, but he
delights in those who have integrity.

You can be sure that evil people will be punished, but
the children of the godly will go free.

PROVERBS 11:20-21, NLT

How can a young person stay pure?

By obeying your word and following its rules.

PSALM 119:9, NLT

For God has not called us to impurity but to consecration
[to dedicate ourselves to the most thorough purity].

1 THESSALONIANS 4:7, AMP

SET BOUNDARIES FOR YOURSELF

If you don't ram a stake into the ground and declare, "This is as
far as I go, and I won't go any further," then you'll lose your footing
on the slippery slope of sex. It's amazing how easily we can make
sweeping rationalizations for our behavior:

- "It's okay because I really love her. I *know* I'm going to
  marry her anyway."

- "Why wait until marriage? We're already married in our hearts."
- "Sex isn't wrong for everyone. God is really concerned only about adultery."

Maybe you've said the same things to yourself...the same things that non-Christians say to themselves! That alone should make you feel a bit uncomfortable.

—adapted from Every Young Man's Battle

Because we have these promises, dear friends, let us cleanse ourselves from everything that can defile our body or spirit. And let us work toward complete purity because we fear God.

2 CORINTHIANS 7:1, NLT

As I said when I left for Macedonia, please stay there in Ephesus and try to stop the men who are teaching such wrong doctrine. Put an end to their myths and fables, and their idea of being saved by finding favor with an endless chain of angels leading up to God—wild ideas that stir up questions and arguments instead of helping people accept God's plan of faith. What I am eager for is that all the Christians there will be filled with love that comes from pure hearts, and that their minds will be clean and their faith strong.

1 TIMOTHY 1:3-5, TLB

Do not lay hands on anyone hastily, nor share in other people's sins; keep yourself pure.

1 TIMOTHY 5:22, NKJV

Yes, dear friends, we are already God's children, and we can't even imagine what we will be like when Christ returns. But we do know that when he comes we will be like him, for we will see him as he really is. And all who believe this will keep themselves pure, just as Christ is pure.

1 JOHN 3:2-3, NLT

Finally, brothers, whatever is true, whatever is noble, whatever is right, whatever is pure, whatever is lovely, whatever is admirable—if anything is excellent or praiseworthy— think about such things. Whatever you have learned or received or heard from me, or seen in me—put it into practice. And the God of peace will be with you.

PHILIPPIANS 4:8-9, NIV

God wants the best for you

God's love for you is unconditional; it never changes. Before you were formed in the womb, He loved you. You're the apple of His eye. His love for you has no limits, and His love for you never wanes. When you couldn't put your porn magazines down, He still loved you. When you lay in the arms of another Saturday night date, He still loved you. When you continued to ignore Him, He chased you desperately, aching to reach you before it was too late and your heart had hardened.

—*adapted from* **Every Young Man's Battle**

GOD CAN BE TRUSTED

Blessed is the man who trusts in the LORD,
And whose hope is the LORD.
For he shall be like a tree planted by the waters…
And will not fear when heat comes.

JEREMIAH 17:7,8, NKJV

The LORD is my light and my salvation—
whom shall I fear?
The LORD is the stronghold of my life—
of whom shall I be afraid?

PSALM 27:1, NIV

The LORD looks down from heaven
and sees the whole human race.

From his throne he observes
> all who live on the earth.
He made their hearts,
> so he understands everything they do.

PSALM 33:13-15, NLT

Trust in him at all times; ye people, pour out your heart before him: God is a refuge for us.

PSALM 62:8, KJV

Many sorrows come to the wicked,
> but unfailing love surrounds those who trust
> the LORD.

PSALM 32:10, NLT

HIS COMMANDMENTS ARE BASED IN LOVE

For all God's words are right, and everything he does is worthy of our trust. He loves whatever is just and good; the earth is filled with his tender love.

PSALM 33:4-5, TLB

The precepts of the LORD are right, rejoicing the heart;
The commandment of the LORD is pure, enlightening
> the eyes.

PSALM 19:8, NASB

HAVE FAITH THAT GOD HAS A SPECIAL PERSON WAITING FOR YOU

If you believe, you will receive whatever you ask for in prayer.

MATTHEW 21:22, NLT

Jesus said to him, "If you can believe, all things are possible to him who believes."

MARK 9:23, NKJV

He did not waver at the promise of God through unbelief, but was strengthened in faith, giving glory to God, and being fully convinced that what He had promised He was also able to perform.

ROMANS 4:20-21, NKJV

respect your body

YOUR BODY IS A TEMPLE

Do you not know that you are a temple of God and that
the Spirit of God dwells in you?

1 CORINTHIANS 3:16, NASB

Do you not know that your bodies are members of Christ?
Shall I therefore take the members of Christ and make
them members of a prostitute? Never! Do you not know
that he who joins himself to a prostitute becomes one
body with her? For, as it is written, "The two shall become
one." But he who is united to the Lord becomes one spirit
with him.… Do you not know that your body is a temple
of the Holy Spirit within you, which you have from God?
You are not your own; you were bought with a price. So
glorify God in your body.

1 CORINTHIANS 6:15-17,19-20, RSV

And what union can there be between God's temple and
idols? For you are God's temple, the home of the living
God, and God has said of you, "I will live in them and
walk among them, and I will be their God and they shall
be my people."

2 CORINTHIANS 6:16, TLB

I no longer live, but Christ lives in me.

GALATIANS 2:20, NIV

YOU WERE MADE IN THE IMAGE OF GOD

God honored the Master's body by raising it from the grave. He'll treat yours with the same resurrection power. Until that time, remember that your bodies are created with the same dignity as the Master's body. You wouldn't take the Master's body off to a whorehouse, would you? I should hope not.

1 CORINTHIANS 6:15, MSG

There is a sense in which sexual sins are different from all others. In sexual sin we violate the sacredness of our own bodies, these bodies that were made for God-given and God-modeled love, for "becoming one" with another. Or didn't you realize that your body is a sacred place, the place of the Holy Spirit? Don't you see that you can't live however you please, squandering what God paid such a high price for? The physical part of you is not some piece of property belonging to the spiritual part of you. God owns the whole works. So let people see God in and through your body.

1 CORINTHIANS 6:18-20, MSG

YOU ARE PART OF SOMETHING BIGGER

Your body has many parts—limbs, organs, cells—but no matter how many parts you can name, you're still one body. It's exactly the same with Christ. By means of his one Spirit, we all said goodbye to our partial and piecemeal lives. We each used to independently call our own shots, but then we entered into a large and integrated life in which he has the final say in everything. (This is what we proclaimed in word and action when we were baptized.) Each of us is now a part of his resurrection body, refreshed and sustained at one fountain—his Spirit—where we all come to drink. The old labels we once used to identify ourselves—labels like Jew or Greek, slave or free—are no longer useful. We need something larger, more comprehensive.

I want you to think about how all this makes you more significant, not less. A body isn't just a single part blown up into something huge. It's all the different-but-similar parts arranged and functioning together. If Foot said, "I'm not elegant like Hand, embellished with rings; I guess I don't belong to this body," would that make it so? If Ear said, "I'm not beautiful like Eye, limpid and expressive; I don't deserve a place on the head," would you want to remove it from the body? If the body was all eye, how could it hear? If all ear, how could it smell? As it is, we see that God has carefully placed each part of the body right where he wanted it.

But I also want you to think about how this keeps your significance from getting blown up into self-importance. For no matter how significant you are, it is only because of what you are a part of. An enormous eye or a gigantic hand wouldn't be a body, but a monster. What we have is one body with many parts, each its proper size and in its proper place. No part is important on its own. Can you imagine Eye telling Hand, "Get lost; I don't need you"? Or, Head telling Foot, "You're fired; your job has been phased out"? As a matter of fact, in practice it works the other way—the "lower" the part, the more basic, and therefore necessary. You can live without an eye, for instance, but not without a stomach. When it's a part of your own body you are concerned with, it makes no difference whether the part is visible or clothed, higher or lower. You give it dignity and honor just as it is, without comparisons. If anything, you have more concern for the lower parts than the higher. If you had to choose, wouldn't you prefer good digestion to full-bodied hair?

The way God designed our bodies is a model for understanding our lives together as a church: every part dependent on every other part, the parts we mention and the parts we don't, the parts we see and the parts we don't. If one part hurts, every other part is involved in the hurt, and in the healing. If one part flourishes, every other part enters into the exuberance.

You are Christ's body—that's who you are! You must never forget this. Only as you accept your part of that body does your "part" mean anything.

1 CORINTHIANS 12:12-27, MSG

THE BOTTOM LINE ON WHAT'S OUT OF BOUNDS

The LORD said to Moses, "Speak to the Israelites and say to them: 'I am the LORD your God. You must not do as they do in Egypt, where you used to live, and you must not do as they do in the land of Canaan, where I am bringing you. Do not follow their practices. You must obey my laws and be careful to follow my decrees. I am the LORD your God. Keep my decrees and laws, for the man who obeys them will live by them. I am the LORD.

"'No one is to approach any close relative to have sexual relations. I am the LORD.

"'Do not dishonor your father by having sexual relations with your mother. She is your mother; do not have relations with her.

"'Do not have sexual relations with your father's wife; that would dishonor your father.

"'Do not have sexual relations with your sister, either your father's daughter or your mother's daughter, whether she was born in the same home or elsewhere.

"'Do not have sexual relations with your son's daughter or your daughter's daughter; that would dishonor you.

"'Do not have sexual relations with the daughter of your father's wife, born to your father; she is your sister.

"'Do not have sexual relations with your father's sister; she is your father's close relative.

" 'Do not have sexual relations with your mother's sister, because she is your mother's close relative.

" 'Do not dishonor your father's brother by approaching his wife to have sexual relations; she is your aunt.

" 'Do not have sexual relations with your daughter-in-law. She is your son's wife; do not have relations with her.

" 'Do not have sexual relations with your brother's wife; that would dishonor your brother.

" 'Do not have sexual relations with both a woman and her daughter. Do not have sexual relations with either her son's daughter or her daughter's daughter; they are her close relatives. That is wickedness.

" 'Do not take your wife's sister as a rival wife and have sexual relations with her while your wife is living.

" 'Do not approach a woman to have sexual relations during the uncleanness of her monthly period.

" 'Do not have sexual relations with your neighbor's wife and defile yourself with her.

" 'Do not give any of your children to be sacrificed to Molech, for you must not profane the name of your God. I am the LORD.

" 'Do not lie with a man as one lies with a woman; that is detestable.

" 'Do not have sexual relations with an animal and defile yourself with it. A woman must not present herself to an animal to have sexual relations with it; that is a perversion.

" 'Do not defile yourselves in any of these ways, because this is how the nations that I am going to drive out before you became defiled. Even the land was defiled; so I punished it for its sin, and the land vomited out its inhabitants. But you must keep my decrees and my laws. The native-born and the aliens living among you must not do any of these detestable things, for all these things were done by the people who lived in the land before you, and the land became defiled. And if you defile the land, it will vomit you out as it vomited out the nations that were before you.

" 'Everyone who does any of these detestable things— such persons must be cut off from their people. Keep my requirements and do not follow any of the detestable customs that were practiced before you came and do not defile yourselves with them. I am the LORD your God.' "

LEVITICUS 18:1-29, NIV

treat her with the honor she deserves

SHOW REAL LOVE FOR HER

Teenage guys often try to justify sex outside of marriage, saying, "But we love each other! That's why it felt so right for us to sleep together!" But true love for your neighbor (or your girlfriend) can only exist and can only be expressed through obedience to God's standards. Anything less is counterfeit love.

> Everyone who believes that Jesus is the Christ is born of God, and everyone who loves the father loves his child as well. This is how we know that we love the children of God [in this case, your girlfriend]: by loving God and carrying out his commands.
>
> 1 JOHN 5:1-2, NIV

> Since by your obedience to the Truth through the [Holy] Spirit you have purified your hearts for the sincere affection of the brethren, [see that you] love one another fervently from a pure heart.
>
> 1 PETER 1:22, AMP

> This is his command: to believe in the name of his Son, Jesus Christ, and to love one another as he commanded us. Those who obey his commands live in him, and he in them.
>
> JOHN 3:23-24, NIV

If there's anywhere we need to be authentic, it's in our relation-ships with girls. You must leave her better than when you met her. So are you going to do that?

—Every Young Man's Battle

Honor all people, love the brotherhood, fear God.

1 PETER 2:17, NASB

We know what real love is because Christ gave up his life for us. And so we also ought to give up our lives for our Christian brothers and sisters.

1 JOHN 3:16, NLT

And God himself has said that one must love not only God, but his brother too.

1 JOHN 4:21, TLB

DON'T TRY TO PUSH PAST HER BOUNDARIES

In the days of the prophet Ezekiel, God's people—Israel—had strayed again, committing "adultery" against Him by chasing other gods. The Lord sought a metaphor that He could use through Ezekiel that could help us understand the depth of their sin and would express to His people how deeply they had hurt Him. He wanted to find something that was clearly despicable and clearly wrong to which to compare this sin. He chose premarital petting, or groping, as the comparison, clearly revealing His thoughts and attitudes about the topic: petting is just as bad as choosing other gods over Him!

> In that land their breasts were fondled and their virgin
> bosoms caressed.
>
> EZEKIEL 23:3, NIV

When you push past your girlfriend's sexual boundaries and standards, you break Christian unity with her. You also break unity with God.

> If your [girlfriend] is distressed because of what you [ask
> her to do sexually], you are no longer acting in love. Do
> not by your [sexual requests] destroy your [girlfriend] for
> whom Christ died.… For the kingdom of God is not a mat-
> ter of [parking or groping or pushing past your girlfriend's
> boundaries], but of righteousness, peace and joy in the Holy
> Spirit, because anyone who serves Christ in this way is
> pleasing to God and approved by men.
>   Let us therefore make every effort to do what leads
> to peace and to mutual edification [unity in Christ].
> Do not destroy the work of God for the sake of [parking
> or groping or pushing past your girlfriend's boundaries].
>
> ROMANS 14:15,17-20, NIV
>
> *(Author's wording in brackets)*

Treat…younger women as sisters, with absolute purity.

1 TIMOTHY 5:1-2, NIV

EVALUATE YOUR DEFINITION OF BEAUTY

A story from Fred Stoeker:

"Amy, seventeen years old, exclaimed, 'I just finished your book *Every Young Man's Battle.* Wow! I had no idea how much what I do and what I wear affects the young men around me. I have always had high standards for modest clothes, but now they will be even higher.'

"Although it's natural to be distracted and even attracted by a young woman in revealing clothes, the Bible tells us that true beauty comes from a pure heart. Amy's amazing response, her desire to respect those around her, reflects the kind of beauty that endures. What kind of woman will attract your attention: one who flaunts her body to every guy who walks by or one who chooses to focus on inner beauty and to reserve her body solely for her husband?

"Reexamine your definitions of beauty, and let your girlfriend know that you appreciate her helping you toward purity by dressing modestly."

And I want women to be modest in their appearance.
They should wear decent and appropriate clothing and not
draw attention to themselves by the way they fix their hair

or by wearing gold or pearls or expensive clothes. For women who claim to be devoted to God should make themselves attractive by the good things they do.

1 TIMOTHY 2:9-10, NLT

[Addressed to women] Don't be concerned about the outward beauty that depends on jewelry, or beautiful clothes, or hair arrangement. Be beautiful inside, in your hearts, with the lasting charm of a gentle and quiet spirit which is so precious to God. That kind of deep beauty was seen in the saintly women of old, who trusted God and fitted in with their husbands' plans.

1 PETER 3:3-5, TLB

GOD WANTS YOU TO RESPECT HER FATHER

A message from Fred Stoeker:

"I know you're my Christian brother, so I want to count on you to stand shoulder to shoulder with me in this call I have from God to keep my daughter pure until marriage. Yes, I'm in my early forties and you may be in your teens or early twenties, but I'm as much your brother as your buddies are, and I'm counting on you not to lay your hands on my daughter just as much as your best friend is counting on you not to lay your hands on his girlfriend. Honor me in this."

—*adapted from* **Every Young Man's Battle**

The rich man owned many sheep and cattle. The poor
man owned nothing but a little lamb he had worked hard
to buy. He raised that little lamb, and it grew up with his
children. It ate from the man's own plate and drank from
his cup. He cuddled it in his arms like a baby daughter.
One day a guest arrived at the home of the rich man. But
instead of killing a lamb from his own flocks for food, he
took the poor man's lamb and killed it and served it to
his guest.

2 SAMUEL 12:2-4, NLT

…but a true friend sticks by you like family.

PROVERBS 18:24, MSG

Lord, who may dwell in your sanctuary?
    Who may live on your holy hill?
He…who keeps his oath, even when it hurts.

PSALM 15:1,4, NIV

marriage is worth waiting for

THE BIBLICAL BASIS FOR MARRIAGE—AND SEX

So God created people in his own image;
    God patterned them after himself;
    male and female he created them.
God blessed them and told them, "Multiply and fill the
      earth...."

GENESIS 1:27-28, NLT

And the Lord God said, "It isn't good for man to be alone;
I will make a companion for him, a helper suited to his
needs."

GENESIS 2:18, TLB

Therefore a man leaves his father and his mother and
cleaves to his wife, and they become one flesh. And the
man and his wife were both naked, and were not ashamed.

GENESIS 2:24-25, RSV

"Haven't you read the Scriptures?" Jesus replied. "They
record that from the beginning 'God made them male and
female.' And he said, 'This explains why a man leaves his
father and mother and is joined to his wife, and the two
are united into one.' Since they are no longer two but one,
let no one separate them, for God has joined them
together."

MATTHEW 19:4-6, NLT

GOD PURPOSEFULLY RESERVED SEX FOR MARRIAGE

A story from a young woman:

"When we started dating fourteen months ago, everything was perfect. I felt I'd finally met a great Christian guy who loved my family and agreed with my morals. But six months ago, we slept together. We were both virgins and, to tell you the truth, I didn't want to do it. I had struggled through many relationships before and had remained pure. I was so wanting to wait for my wedding night, but I also wanted to make him happy, so I let it go too far.

"Since then, life has been terrible. I knew that getting it on was a mistake and a sin before I even did it, but the experience really hit him hard too. Now every other area of his life has been impacted. He doesn't think looking at pornography is wrong, he doesn't think cursing is wrong, he doesn't think premarital sex is wrong, and he doesn't even honor his parents or mine anymore. We were thinking about getting married after college, but now I don't know what to do. He views everything I say as 'nagging.' I just want the same godly man back that I grew to love. I guess I don't want to face the fact that this man that I gave myself to is not the one who God has planned for me to marry."

—*adapted from* **Every Young Man's Battle**

Is it a good thing to have sexual relations?

Certainly—but only within a certain context. It's good for a man to have a wife, and for a woman to have a husband. Sexual drives are strong, but marriage is strong

enough to contain them and provide for a balanced and fulfilling sexual life in a world of sexual disorder. The marriage
bed must be a place of mutuality—the husband seeking to
satisfy his wife, the wife seeking to satisfy her husband. Marriage is not a place to "stand up for your rights." Marriage is
a decision to serve the other, whether in bed or out.

1 CORINTHIANS 7:1-4, MSG

Give honor to marriage, and remain faithful to one
another in marriage. God will surely judge people who are
immoral and those who commit adultery.

HEBREWS 13:4, NLT

And he answered and said unto them, Have ye not read,
that he which made them at the beginning made them
male and female, and said, For this cause shall a man leave
father and mother, and shall cleave to his wife: and they
twain shall be one flesh? Wherefore they are no more
twain, but one flesh. What therefore God hath joined
together, let not man put asunder.

MATTHEW 19:4-6, KJV

THE BENEFITS OF A GOOD WIFE ARE HARD TO BEAT

Let your wife be a fountain of blessing for you. Rejoice in
the wife of your youth. She is a loving doe, a graceful deer.

Let her breasts satisfy you always. May you always be captivated by her love.

PROVERBS 5:18-19, NLT

Enjoy life with the wife whom you love, all the days of your vain life which he has given you under the sun, because that is your portion in life.

ECCLESIASTES 9:9, RSV

House and wealth are an inheritance from fathers,
But a prudent wife is from the LORD.

PROVERBS 19:14, NASB

He who finds a wife finds a good thing,
And obtains favor from the LORD.

PROVERBS 18:22, NKJV

My lover is to me a cluster of henna blossoms
from the vineyards of En Gedi.
How beautiful you are, my darling!
Oh, how beautiful!
Your eyes are doves.

SONG OF SONGS 1:14-15, NIV

A wife of noble character who can find?
She is worth far more than rubies.

PROVERBS 31:10, NIV

LOVE IS MUCH MORE THAN GETTING PHYSICAL

But God demonstrates his own love for us in this: While
we were still sinners, Christ died for us.

ROMANS 5:8, NIV

Love is very patient and kind, never jealous or envious,
never boastful or proud, never haughty or selfish or rude.
Love does not demand its own way. It is not irritable or
touchy. It does not hold grudges and will hardly even
notice when others do it wrong.

1 CORINTHIANS 13:4-5, TLB

Hatred stirs up strife,
But love covers all sins.

PROVERBS 10:12, NKJV

Love never gives up, never loses faith, is always hopeful,
and endures through every circumstance.

1 CORINTHIANS 13:7, NLT

My command is this: Love each other as I have loved you.

JOHN 15:12, NIV

In this same way, husbands ought to love their wives as
their own bodies. He who loves his wife loves himself.

After all, no one ever hated his own body, but he feeds and cares for it, just as Christ does the church—for we are members of his body. "For this reason a man will leave his father and mother and be united to his wife, and the two will become one flesh."

EPHESIANS 5:28-31, NIV

THE ADVANTAGES OF BEING SINGLE

I want you to live as free of complications as possible. When you're unmarried, you're free to concentrate on simply pleasing the Master. Marriage involves you in all the nuts and bolts of domestic life and in wanting to please your spouse, leading to so many more demands on your attention. The time and energy that married people spend on caring for and nurturing each other, the unmarried can spend in becoming whole and holy instruments of God. I'm trying to be helpful and make it as easy as possible for you, not making things harder. All I want is for you to be able to develop a way of life in which you can spend plenty of time together with the Master without a lot of distractions.

1 CORINTHIANS 7:32-35, MSG

I…tell the unmarried…that singleness might well be the best thing for them, as it has been for me [Paul].

1 CORINTHIANS 7:8, MSG

I would like you to be free from concern. An unmarried man is concerned about the Lord's affairs—how he can please the Lord.... I am saying this for your own good, not to restrict you, but that you may live in a right way in undivided devotion to the Lord.

1 CORINTHIANS 7:32,35, NIV

if it feels so right,
how can it be wrong?

GOD COMMANDS US TO BE HOLY

For I am the LORD your God; consecrate yourselves therefore, and be holy, for I am holy.… For I am the LORD who
brought you up out of the land of Egypt, to be your God;
you shall therefore be holy, for I am holy.

LEVITICUS 11:44-45, RSV

Say to all the assembly of the Israelites, You shall be holy,
for I the Lord your God am holy.

LEVITICUS 19:2, AMP

Since you have…learned the truth that is in Jesus,
throw off your old evil nature and your former way of
life, which is rotten through and through, full of lust
and deception. Instead, there must be a spiritual renewal
of your thoughts and attitudes. You must display a new
nature because you are a new person, created in God's
likeness—righteous, holy, and true.

EPHESIANS 4:22-24, NLT

But now you must be holy in everything you do, just
as God—who chose you to be his children—is holy.
For he himself has said, "You must be holy because I
am holy."

1 PETER 1:15-16, NLT

To set the mind on the flesh is death, but to set the mind
on the Spirit is life and peace.

ROMANS 8:6, RSV

EVERY CHOICE HAS A CONSEQUENCE

It's critical to recognize visual sexual impurity as foreplay. If viewing
sensual things merely provides a flutter of appreciation for a
woman's beauty, it would be no different than viewing the awesome power of a thunderstorm racing over the Iowa cornfields.
There would be no sin and no problem.

But if it *is* foreplay, and you *are* getting sexual gratification,
then it defiles your body and your relationships. And it's certain
that you'll be paying a cost that you may not even be aware of.

—adapted from Every Young Man's Battle

Do not be deceived: God cannot be mocked. A man reaps
what he sows. The one who sows to please his sinful
nature, from that nature will reap destruction; the one
who sows to please the Spirit, from the Spirit will reap
eternal life.

GALATIANS 6:7-8, NIV

Don't be misled: No one makes a fool of God. What a person plants, he will harvest.

GALATIANS 6:7, MSG

As I have observed, those who plow evil
and those who sow trouble reap it.

JOB 4:8, NIV

They sow the wind
and reap the whirlwind.
The stalk has no head;
it will produce no flour.
Were it to yield grain,
foreigners would swallow it up.

HOSEA 8:7, NIV

What benefit did you reap at that time from the
things you are now ashamed of? Those things result
in death!

ROMANS 6:21, NIV

You can buy an hour with a whore for a loaf of bread,
but a wanton woman may well eat *you* alive.
Can you build a fire in your lap
and not burn your pants?
Can you walk barefoot on hot coals
and not get blisters?
It's the same when you have sex…
Touch her and you'll pay for it. No excuses.

PROVERBS 6:26-29, MSG

The LORD hates people with twisted hearts, but he
      delights in those who have integrity.
You can be sure that evil people will be punished, but
      the children of the godly will go free.

PROVERBS 11:20-21, NLT

Don't you know that those who do wrong will have no
share in the Kingdom of God? Don't fool yourselves.
Those who indulge in sexual sin, who are idol worshipers, adulterers, male prostitutes…none of these will have a
share in the Kingdom of God.

1 CORINTHIANS 6:9-10, NLT

The authorities are sent by God to help you. But if you are
doing something wrong, of course you should be afraid,
for you will be punished. The authorities are established by
God for that very purpose, to punish those who do wrong.

ROMANS 13:4, NLT

But by your hard and impenitent heart you are storing up
wrath for yourself on the day of wrath when God's righteous judgment will be revealed.

ROMANS 2:5, RSV

But my people have stubborn and rebellious hearts. They
have turned against me and have chosen to practice

idolatry. They do not say from the heart, "Let us live in awe of the LORD our God, for he gives us rain each spring and fall, assuring us of plentiful harvests." Your wickedness has deprived you of these wonderful blessings. Your sin has robbed you of all these good things.

JEREMIAH 5:23-25, NLT

I will not answer when they cry for help. Even though they anxiously search for me, they will not find me. For they hated knowledge and chose not to fear the LORD. They rejected my advice and paid no attention when I corrected them. That is why they must eat the bitter fruit of living their own way. They must experience the full terror of the path they have chosen.

PROVERBS 1:28-31, NLT

So I advise you to live according to your new life in the Holy Spirit. Then you won't be doing what your sinful nature craves. The old sinful nature loves to do evil, which is just opposite from what the Holy Spirit wants. And the Spirit gives us desires that are opposite from what the sinful nature desires. These two forces are constantly fighting each other, and your choices are never free from this conflict. But when you are directed by the Holy Spirit, you are no longer subject to the law.

When you follow the desires of your sinful nature, your lives will produce these evil results: sexual immorality, impure thoughts, eagerness for lustful pleasure, idolatry, participation in demonic activities, hostility, quarreling, jealousy, outbursts of anger, selfish ambition, divisions, the feeling that everyone is wrong except those in your own little group, envy, drunkenness, wild parties, and other kinds of sin. Let me tell you again…that anyone living that sort of life will not inherit the Kingdom of God.

GALATIANS 5:16-21, NLT

FREEDOM COMES WITH RESPONSIBILITY

A lot of us talk a good game about purity while sitting on the bench (or sitting in church), but when given the chance to play, we keep our eyes on the babes in the stands, not on the pitcher holding the ball.

If you aren't trustworthy in handling fleshly passions, how can you be trusted to handle things of greater value?

—*adapted from* Every Young Man's Battle

Be careful with this freedom of yours. Do not cause a brother or sister with a weaker conscience to stumble.

1 CORINTHIANS 8:9, NLT

For you have been called to live in freedom—not freedom to satisfy your sinful nature, but freedom to serve one another in love.

GALATIANS 5:13, NLT

In this matter no one should wrong his brother or take advantage of him. The Lord will punish men for all such sins, as we have already told you and warned you.

1 THESSALONIANS 4:6, NIV

Live as free men, yet without using your freedom as a pretext for evil; but live as servants of God.

1 PETER 2:16, RSV

You may say, "I am allowed to do anything." But I reply, "Not everything is good for you." And even though "I am allowed to do anything," I must not become a slave to anything.

1 CORINTHIANS 6:12, NLT

You say, "I am allowed to do anything"—but not everything is helpful. You say, "I am allowed to do anything"—but not everything is beneficial.

1 CORINTHIANS 10:23, NLT

It is obvious what kind of life develops out of trying to get your own way all the time: repetitive, loveless, cheap sex; a stinking accumulation of mental and emotional garbage; frenzied and joyless grabs for happiness; trinket gods; magic-show religion; paranoid loneliness; cutthroat competition; all-consuming-yet-never-satisfied wants; a brutal temper; an impotence to love or be loved; divided homes and divided lives; small-minded and lopsided pursuits; the vicious habit of depersonalizing everyone into a rival; uncontrolled and uncontrollable addictions; ugly parodies of community. I could go on.

This isn't the first time I have warned you, you know. If you use your freedom this way, you will not inherit God's kingdom.

GALATIANS 5:19-21, MSG

WHAT'S MORE IMPORTANT, PURITY OR PLEASURE?

James, a respected teen in his youth group, refused to promise to stay sexually pure when pressed to do so. "There are too many unforeseen situations out there for me to make such a promise," he said. Translation: "I want to keep my options open."

James has stopped short. Have you?

—*adapted from* Every Young Man's Battle

For those who live according to the flesh set their minds on the things of the flesh, but those who live according to the Spirit, the things of the Spirit.

ROMANS 8:5, NKJV

Let not sin therefore reign in your mortal bodies, to make you obey their passions.

ROMANS 6:12, RSV

I want you to promise, O women of Jerusalem, not to
awaken love until the time is right.

SONG OF SOLOMON 8:4, NLT

A spiritual battle for purity is going on in every heart and soul. The
costs are real. Obedience is hard, requiring humility and meekness,
very rare elements indeed.

—Every Young Man's Battle

Among these we all once lived in the passions of our flesh,
following the desires of body and mind, and so we were by
nature children of wrath, like the rest of mankind. But God,
who is rich in mercy, out of the great love with which he
loved us, even when we were dead through our trespasses,
made us alive together with Christ (by grace you have been
saved)…that in the coming ages he might show the
immeasurable riches of his grace in kindness toward us in
Christ Jesus.

EPHESIANS 2:3-5,7, RSV

So kill (deaden, deprive of power) the evil desire lurking in
your members [those animal impulses and all that is
earthly in you that is employed in sin]: sexual vice, impurity, sensual appetites, unholy desires, and all greed and
covetousness, for that is idolatry (the deifying of self and
other created things instead of God).

COLOSSIANS 3:5, AMP

Now flee from youthful lusts and pursue righteousness,
faith, love and peace, with those who call on the Lord
from a pure heart.

2 TIMOTHY 2:22, NASB

But flee from these things, you man of God, and pursue
righteousness, godliness, faith, love, perseverance and
gentleness.

1 TIMOTHY 6:11, NASB

As we know Jesus better, his divine power gives us
everything we need for living a godly life. He has called us
to receive his own glory and goodness! And by that same
mighty power, he has given us all of his rich and wonderful
promises. He has promised that you will escape the deca-
dence all around you caused by evil desires and that you
will share in his divine nature.

2 PETER 1:3-4, NLT

PURITY STARTS IN THE MIND

You can feel a new light and lightness in your soul when you turn
from sexual sin. Along with inner peace comes an outer peace
that will affect your daily life.

—adapted from Every Man's Battle

To the pure all things are pure, but to the corrupt and

unbelieving nothing is pure; their very minds and consciences are corrupted.

TITUS 1:15, RSV

You will keep in perfect peace
    him whose mind is steadfast,
    because he trusts in you.

ISAIAH 26:3, NIV

You've got a decision to make. You can't visually feed on the same
films as your school chums and expect to stay sexually pure. Do
you want sexual purity and deeper intimacy with God that follows,
or do you want to be one of the gang, squeezing in purity only
when it's convenient?

—*adapted from* Every Young Man's Battle

Be careful. If you're thinking, "Oh, I would never behave
like that"—let this be a warning to you. For you too may
fall into sin.

1 CORINTHIANS 10:12, TLB

Those who live according to the sinful nature have their
minds set on what that nature desires; but those who live
in accordance with the Spirit have their minds set on what
the Spirit desires. The mind of sinful man is death, but the
mind controlled by the Spirit is life and peace.

ROMANS 8:5-6, NIV

Do not be conformed to this world but be transformed by the renewal of your mind, that you may prove what is the will of God, what is good and acceptable and perfect.

ROMANS 12:2, RSV

A CLEAR CONSCIENCE LEADS TO TRUE HAPPINESS

I will maintain my innocence without wavering. My conscience is clear for as long as I live.

JOB 27:6, NLT

Paul, looking intently at the Council, said, "Brethren, I have lived my life with a perfectly good conscience before God up to this day."

ACTS 23:1, NASB

I am speaking the truth in Christ, I am not lying; my conscience bears me witness in the Holy Spirit.

ROMANS 9:1, RSV

But the goal of our instruction is love from a pure heart and a good conscience and a sincere faith.

1 TIMOTHY 1:5, NASB

We are so glad that we can say with utter honesty that in all our dealings we have been pure and sincere, quietly depending upon the Lord for his help, and not on our own skills. And that is even more true, if possible, about the way we have acted toward you.

2 CORINTHIANS 1:12, TLB

But if you're breaking the rules right and left, watch out. The police aren't there just to be admired in their uniforms. God also has an interest in keeping order, and he uses them to do it. That's why you must live responsibly— not just to avoid punishment but also because it's the right way to live.

ROMANS 13:4-5, MSG

Therefore, it is necessary to submit to the authorities, not only because of possible punishment but also because of conscience.

ROMANS 13:5, NIV

who will you listen to?

It's obvious that if you want to stay in control, you have to set your rules, choose carefully who you do things with, and stay disciplined.

—*adapted from* **Every Young Man's Battle**

DO YOUR FRIENDS ENCOURAGE YOU TO MAKE GOOD CHOICES?

So often there's no challenging voice calling us to obedience and authenticity. Instead, we move nearer to our peers, often sitting together on the middle ground, a good distance from God. When challenged by His higher standards, we're comforted that we don't look too different from other Christians around us. Trouble is, we don't look much different from non-Christians either.

—**Every Young Man's Battle**

I have written you in my letter not to associate with sexually immoral people…. But now I am writing you that you must not associate with anyone who calls himself a brother but is sexually immoral or greedy, an idolater or a slanderer, a drunkard or a swindler. With such a man do not even eat.

1 CORINTHIANS 5:9,11, NIV

Don't be teamed with those who do not love the Lord, for what do the people of God have in common with the people of sin? How can light live with darkness?

And what harmony can there be between Christ and
the devil?

2 CORINTHIANS 6:14-15, TLB

Now we command you, brethren, in the name of our Lord
Jesus Christ, that you keep away from every brother who
leads an unruly life and not according to the tradition
which you received from us.

2 THESSALONIANS 3:6, NASB

And have no fellowship with the unfruitful works of darkness, but rather expose them.

EPHESIANS 5:11, NKJV

HANGING OUT WITH FOOLS LEADS TO DISASTER

Stay away from fools, for you won't find knowledge there.
The wise look ahead to see what is coming, but fools
deceive themselves.

PROVERBS 14:7-8, NLT

O my son, be wise and stay in God's paths; don't carouse
with drunkards and gluttons, for they are on their way to
poverty.

PROVERBS 23:19-20, TLB

The wise man is glad to be instructed, but a self-sufficient fool falls flat on his face.

PROVERBS 10:8, TLB

Men of perverse heart shall be far from me;
I will have nothing to do with evil.

PSALM 101:4, NIV

Fools think they need no advice, but the wise listen to others.

PROVERBS 12:15, NLT

The crown of the wise is their riches,
But the folly of fools is foolishness.

PROVERBS 14:24, NASB

A wise person thinks much about death, while the fool thinks only about having a good time now.

ECCLESIASTES 7:4, NLT

The righteous will never be removed,
But the wicked will not inhabit the earth.

PROVERBS 10:30, NKJV

For they mouth empty, boastful words and, by appealing to the lustful desires of sinful human nature, they entice people who are just escaping from those who live in error. They promise them freedom, while they themselves are slaves of depravity—for a man is a slave to whatever has mastered him.

2 PETER 2:18-19, NIV

Good people are guided by their honesty; treacherous people are destroyed by their dishonesty.

PROVERBS 11:3, NLT

The heart of the wise inclines to the right,
   but the heart of the fool to the left.

ECCLESIASTES 10:2, NIV

But there were also false prophets in Israel, just as there will be false teachers among you. They will cleverly teach their destructive heresies about God and even turn against their Master who bought them. Theirs will be a swift and terrible end.

2 PETER 2:1, NLT

Their future is eternal destruction. Their god is their appetite, they brag about shameful things, and all they think about is this life here on earth.

PHILIPPIANS 3:19, NLT

Words from a wise man's mouth are gracious,
   but a fool is consumed by his own lips.

ECCLESIASTES 10:12, NIV

ARE YOU BRINGING HONOR TO YOUR PARENTS?

A wise child brings joy to a father; a foolish child brings grief to a mother.

PROVERBS 10:1, NLT

A sensible son gladdens his father. A rebellious son saddens his mother.

PROVERBS 15:20, TLB

A wise son makes his father happy, but a lad who hangs around with prostitutes disgraces him.

PROVERBS 29:3, TLB

He who becomes the parent of a [self-confident] fool does it to his sorrow, and the father of [an empty-headed] fool has no joy [in him].

PROVERBS 17:21, AMP

Whoso keepeth the law is a wise son: but he that is a companion of riotous men shameth his father.

PROVERBS 28:7, KJV

The father of godly children has cause for joy. What a pleasure it is to have wise children. So give your parents joy! May she who gave you birth be happy.

PROVERBS 23:24-25, NLT

FIND FRIENDS WHO WILL HELP YOU STAND STRONG

The way of the righteous is like the first gleam of dawn,
which shines ever brighter until the full light of day.

PROVERBS 4:18, NLT

Blessed are the undefiled in the way,
Who walk in the law of the LORD!

PSALM 119:1, NKJV

For the wicked shall be cut off;
  but those who wait for the LORD shall possess the
    land.
The righteous shall possess the land,
  and dwell upon it for ever.

PSALM 37:9,29, RSV

Follow the steps of good men instead, and stay on the
paths of the righteous. For only the upright will live in the
land, and those who have integrity will remain in it. But
the wicked will be removed from the land, and the treacherous will be destroyed.

PROVERBS 2:20-22, NLT

The words of the wise heard in quiet are better than the
shouting of a ruler among fools.

ECCLESIASTES 9:17, RSV

Although a wicked man commits a hundred crimes and
still lives a long time, I know that it will go better with
God-fearing men, who are reverent before God.

ECCLESIASTES 8:12, NIV

When I [Paul] wrote to you before, I told you not to associate with people who indulge in sexual sin.

1 CORINTHIANS 5:9, NLT

LISTEN TO THE WISDOM OF YOUR COMMANDER, SOLDIER

My son, do not forget my teaching,
But let your heart keep my commandments;
For length of days and years of life
And peace they will add to you.
Do not let kindness and truth leave you;
Bind them around your neck,
Write them on the tablet of your heart.
So you will find favor and good repute
In the sight of God and man.

PROVERBS 3:1-4, NASB

My son, keep my words
And treasure my commandments within you.
Keep my commandments and live,
And my teaching as the apple of your eye.

PROVERBS 7:1-2, NASB

Acquire wisdom! Acquire understanding!
Do not forget nor turn away from the words of my
     mouth.

PROVERBS 4:5, NASB

Love the LORD your God,…walk in his ways, and…keep
his commands, decrees and laws; then you will live and
increase, and the LORD your God will bless you in the land
you are entering to possess.

DEUTERONOMY 30:16, NIV

But the good man walks along in the ever-brightening
light of God's favor; the dawn gives way to morning splen-
dor, while the evil man gropes and stumbles in the dark.
     Listen, son of mine, to what I say. Listen carefully.
Keep these thoughts ever in mind; let them penetrate deep
within your heart, for they will mean real life for you, and
radiant health.

PROVERBS 4:18-22, TLB

Hear, my son, and receive my sayings,
And the years of your life will be many.

PROVERBS 4:10, NKJV

With long life I will satisfy him,
And show him My salvation.

PSALM 91:16, NKJV

are you committed to the battle?

Tyson tells it exactly like it is, declaring, "It's no secret. Most guys just want to have sex or get some kind of action. They don't care about the relationship part of things, like the girls do. Guys like to see girls with little or nothing on, that's the bottom line. Even us Christian guys."

Even us Christian guys. Hmm. No surprise there. Many Christians will tell you that the thing that surprises them most about being a Christian is that so few live any differently than anyone else in the world.

—adapted from Every Young Man's Battle

DON'T BE DECEIVED BY THE WISDOM OF THE WORLD

Claiming themselves to be wise without God, they
became utter fools instead. And then, instead of worship-
ing the glorious, ever-living God, they took wood and
stone and made idols for themselves, carving them
to look like mere birds and animals and snakes and
puny men.

ROMANS 1:22-23, TLB

Do not deceive yourselves. If any one of you thinks he is
wise by the standards of this age, he should become a
"fool" so that he may become wise. For the wisdom of this
world is foolishness in God's sight.

1 CORINTHIANS 3:18-19, NIV

But avoid worldly and empty chatter, for it will lead to further ungodliness, and their talk will spread like gangrene. Among them are Hymenaeus and Philetus, men who have gone astray from the truth saying that the resurrection has already taken place, and they upset the faith of some.

2 TIMOTHY 2:16-18, NASB

But there were also false prophets in Israel, just as there will be false teachers among you. They will cleverly teach their destructive heresies about God and even turn against their Master who bought them. Theirs will be a swift and terrible end.

2 PETER 2:1, NLT

So the LORD replies to his people, "You love to wander far from me and do not follow in my paths. Now I will no longer accept you as my people. I will remember all your wickedness and will punish you for your sins."

JEREMIAH 14:10, NLT

EXAMINE YOURSELF TO SEE WHERE YOU ARE

Is there a secret, dark side to your Christian image? Are you going on missions trip during the summer but still fondling some girl in the backseat of a car?

—*adapted from* **Every Young Man's Battle**

But let each one examine his own work, and then he will have rejoicing in himself alone, and not in another.

GALATIANS 6:4, NKJV

Examine yourselves to see whether you are in the faith; test yourselves. Do you not realize that Christ Jesus is in you— unless, of course, you fail the test?

2 CORINTHIANS 13:5, NIV

Test me, O LORD, and try me,
    examine my heart and my mind.

PSALM 26:2, NIV

For if you live according to the flesh you will die; but if by the Spirit you put to death the deeds of the body, you will live.

ROMANS 8:13, NKJV

Beloved, if our heart does not condemn us, we have confidence before God; and whatever we ask we receive from Him, because we keep His commandments and do the things that are pleasing in His sight.

1 JOHN 3:21-22, NASB

When you are on your beds,
    search your hearts and be silent.

PSALM 4:4, NIV

PREPARE YOUR MIND FOR BATTLE

Let us behave properly as in the day, not in carousing and
drunkenness, not in sexual promiscuity and sensuality, not
in strife and jealousy. But put on the Lord Jesus Christ,
and make no provision for the flesh in regard to its lusts.

ROMANS 13:13-14, NASB

But take heed to yourselves, lest your hearts be weighed
down with carousing, drunkenness, and cares of this life,
and that Day come on you unexpectedly.

LUKE 21:34, NKJV

And now a personal but most urgent matter; I write in the
gentle but firm spirit of Christ. I hear that I'm being
painted as cringing and wishy-washy when I'm with you,
but harsh and demanding when at a safe distance writing
letters. Please don't force me to take a hard line when I'm
present with you. Don't think that I'll hesitate a single
minute to stand up to those who say I'm an unprincipled
opportunist. Then they'll have to eat their words.

The world is unprincipled. It's dog-eat-dog out there!
The world doesn't fight fair. But we don't live or fight our
battles that way—never have and never will. The tools of
our trade aren't for marketing or manipulation, but they
are for demolishing that entire massively corrupt culture.
We use our powerful God-tools for smashing warped

philosophies, tearing down barriers erected against the truth of God, fitting every loose thought and emotion and impulse into the structure of life shaped by Christ. Our tools are ready at hand for clearing the ground of every obstruction and building lives of obedience into maturity.

2 CORINTHIANS 10:1-11, MSG

So I tell you this, and insist on it in the Lord, that you must no longer live as the Gentiles do, in the futility of their thinking. They are darkened in their understanding and separated from the life of God because of the ignorance that is in them due to the hardening of their hearts. Having lost all sensitivity, they have given themselves over to sensuality so as to indulge in every kind of impurity, with a continual lust for more.

You, however, did not come to know Christ that way. Surely you heard of him and were taught in him in accordance with the truth that is in Jesus. You were taught, with regard to your former way of life, to put off your old self, which is being corrupted by its deceitful desires; to be made new in the attitude of your minds; and to put on the new self, created to be like God in true righteousness and holiness.

EPHESIANS 4:17-24, NIV

Be anxious for nothing, but in everything by prayer and supplication, with thanksgiving, let your requests be made known to God; and the peace of God, which surpasses all understanding, will guard your hearts and minds through Christ Jesus.

PHILIPPIANS 4:6-8, NKJV

And so, dear brothers and sisters who belong to God and are bound for heaven, think about this Jesus whom we declare to be God's Messenger and High Priest.

HEBREWS 3:1, NLT

Keep your eyes on Jesus, our leader and instructor. He was willing to die a shameful death on the cross because of the joy he knew would be his afterwards; and now he sits in the place of honor by the throne of God. If you want to keep from becoming fainthearted and weary, think about his patience as sinful men did such terrible things to him.

HEBREWS 12:2-3, TLB

you've been called to fight

Our heavenly Father exhorts us to be men. He wants us to be like Him. When He calls us to "be perfect as your Father in heaven is perfect," He's asking us to rise above our natural tendencies to impure eyes, fanciful minds, and wandering hearts. While understanding that His standard of purity doesn't come naturally to us, He still calls us to rise up, by the power of His indwelling presence, to get the job done.

Before an important battle for the army he commanded, Joab said to the troops of Israel, "Be of good courage, and let us play the men for our people" (2 Samuel 10:12, KJV). In short, he was saying, "We know God's plan for us. Let's rise up as men, and set our hearts and minds to get it done!"

In the realm of sexual integrity, God wants you to rise up and get it done.

—*adapted from* **Every Man's Battle**

THE COMMAND TO BREAK FREE

We have power through the Lord to overcome every level of sexual immorality, but if we don't utilize that power, we'll never break free of the habit.

—**Every Man's Battle**

> Dearest friends, when I [Paul] was there with you, you were always so careful to follow my instructions. And now that I am away you must be even more careful to do the good things that result from being saved, obeying God

with deep reverence, shrinking back from all that might displease him. For God is at work within you, helping you want to obey him, and then helping you do what he wants.

PHILIPPIANS 2:12-13, TLB

Since you have been raised to new life with Christ, set your sights on the realities of heaven, where Christ sits at God's right hand in the place of honor and power.

COLOSSIANS 3:1, NLT

I will give you a new heart with new and right desires, and I will put a new spirit in you. I will take out your stony heart of sin and give you a new, obedient heart. And I will put my Spirit in you so you will obey my laws and do whatever I command.

EZEKIEL 36:26-27, NLT

No one who is born of God will continue to sin, because God's seed remains in him; he cannot go on sinning, because he has been born of God.

1 JOHN 3:9, NIV

THE COMMAND TO CHOOSE MANHOOD

When it comes down to it, God's definition of real manhood is straightforward and simple: Hear His Word and follow it. That's

God's only definition of manhood—a doer of the Word. And God's definition of a sissy is someone who hears the Word of God and doesn't do it.

—adapted from Every Young Man's Battle

I am speaking in human terms because of the weakness of your flesh. For just as you presented your members as slaves to impurity and to lawlessness, resulting in further lawlessness, so now present your members as slaves to righteousness, resulting in sanctification.

ROMANS 6:19, NASB

Since everything around us is going to melt away, what holy, godly lives you should be living!

2 PETER 3:11, NLT

Therefore do not let sin reign in your mortal body, that you should obey it in its lusts.

ROMANS 6:12, NKJV

THE COMMAND TO COURAGEOUSLY TAKE HOLD OF GOD'S PROVISION

It's like the situation facing Joshua and the people of Israel as they prepared to cross the Jordan River and possess the Promised Land. What did God say to Joshua?

"Have I not commanded you? Be strong and courageous. Do

not be terrified; do not be discouraged, *for the LORD your God will be with you wherever you go*" (Joshua 1:9, [NIV, emphasis added]).

He'd given the Israelites all they needed. They merely had to cross the river.

Regarding sexual purity, God knows the provision He's made for us. We aren't short on power or authority, but what we lack is *urgency*. We must choose to be strong and courageous to walk into purity. In the millisecond it takes to make that choice, the Holy Spirit will start guiding you and walking through the struggle with you.

—Every Man's Battle

Be strong and show yourself a man; keep the charge of the Lord your God, walk in His ways, keep His statutes, His commandments, His precepts, and His testimonies, as it is written in the Law of Moses, that you may do wisely and prosper in all that you do and wherever you turn.

1 KINGS 2:2-3, AMP

Be on your guard; stand firm in the faith; be men of courage; be strong.

1 CORINTHIANS 16:13, NIV

Finally, my brethren, be strong in the Lord, and in the power of his might.

EPHESIANS 6:10, KJV

THE COMMAND TO ABSTAIN

Abstain from all appearance of evil.

1 THESSALONIANS 5:22, KJV

God wants you to be holy, so you should keep clear of all
sexual sin. Then each of you will control your body and
live in holiness and honor—not in lustful passion as the
pagans do, in their ignorance of God and his ways.

1 THESSALONIANS 4:3-5, NLT

Beloved, I urge you as aliens and strangers to abstain from
fleshly lusts which wage war against the soul.

1 PETER 2:11, NASB

But God's truth stands firm like a foundation stone with
this inscription: "The Lord knows those who are his," and
"Those who claim they belong to the Lord must turn away
from all wickedness."

2 TIMOTHY 2:19, NLT

THE COMMAND TO PURIFY YOURSELF

Since we have these promises, dear friends, let us purify
ourselves from everything that contaminates body and
spirit, perfecting holiness out of reverence for God.

2 CORINTHIANS 7:1, NIV

Wash and make yourselves clean.
Take your evil deeds
    out of my sight!
Stop doing wrong.

ISAIAH 1:16, NIV

But in a great house there are not only vessels of gold and silver, but also of wood and clay, some for honor and some for dishonor. Therefore if anyone cleanses himself from the latter, he will be a vessel for honor, sanctified and useful for the Master, prepared for every good work.

2 TIMOTHY 2:20-21, NKJV

Draw near to God and He will draw near to you. Cleanse your hands, you sinners; and purify your hearts.

JAMES 4:8, NASB

THE COMMAND TO LIVE IN A WAY THAT PLEASES GOD

From Fred Stoeker:

"I recall how the Holy Spirit whispered to me, 'This practice can't be tolerated anymore in your life. You are Christ's now, and He loves you.' The implication was that continued sexual activity before marriage would hurt my intimacy with Christ.

When you break His standards, the Lord doesn't reject you, but you can't be as close to Him."

—Every Young Man's Battle

And do not be conformed to this world, but be transformed by the renewing of your mind, that you may
prove what is that good and acceptable and perfect will
of God.

ROMANS 12:2, NKJV

Finally, dear brothers and sisters, we urge you in the name
of the Lord Jesus to live in a way that pleases God, as we
have taught you. You are doing this already, and we
encourage you to do so more and more.

1 THESSALONIANS 4:1, NLT

As obedient children, do not conform to the evil desires
you had when you lived in ignorance. But just as he who
called you is holy, so be holy in all you do.

1 PETER 1:14-15, NIV

As a prisoner for the Lord, then, I urge you to live a life
worthy of the calling you have received.

EPHESIANS 4:1, NIV

You know that we treated each of you as a father treats his
own children. We pleaded with you, encouraged you, and
urged you to live your lives in a way that God would consider worthy.

1 THESSALONIANS 2:11-12, NLT

THE COMMAND TO GROW IN KNOWLEDGE

But grow in the grace and knowledge of our Lord and Savior Jesus Christ. To him be the glory both now and to the day of eternity. Amen.

2 PETER 3:18, RSV

"But let him who boasts boast of this, that he understands and knows Me, that I am the LORD who exercises loving-kindness, justice and righteousness on earth; for I delight in these things," declares the LORD.

JEREMIAH 9:24, NASB

And if you call out for insight
    and cry aloud for understanding,
and if you look for it as for silver
    and search for it as for hidden treasure,
then you will understand the fear of the LORD
    and find the knowledge of God.

PROVERBS 2:3-5, NIV

Happy (blessed, fortunate, enviable) is the man who finds skillful and godly Wisdom, and the man who gets understanding [drawing it forth from God's Word and life's experiences].

PROVERBS 3:13, AMP

But also for this very reason, giving all diligence, add to your faith virtue, to virtue knowledge.

2 PETER 1:5, NKJV

Get wisdom, get understanding: forget it not; neither decline from the words of my mouth.

PROVERBS 4:5, KJV

And you will know the truth, and the truth will set you free.

JOHN 8:32, NLT

THE COMMAND TO FLEE

Flee from sexual immorality. All other sins a man commits are outside his body, but he who sins sexually sins against his own body.

1 CORINTHIANS 6:18, NIV

Now flee from youthful lusts and pursue righteousness, faith, love and peace, with those who call on the Lord from a pure heart.

2 TIMOTHY 2:22, NASB

Run from all these evil things and work instead at what is right and good, learning to trust him and love others, and to be patient and gentle. Fight on for God. Hold tightly to

the eternal life which God has given you, and which you
have confessed with such a ringing confession before many
witnesses.

1 TIMOTHY 6:11-12, TLB

THE COMMAND TO LIVE AS CHILDREN OF THE LIGHT

When given the choice between meeting God's standard and being
accepted by Him, or ignoring those standards and being accepted
by our peers, too many of us choose our peers. We don't really
have the faith that God exists or believe that He'll reward those
who earnestly seek Him.

—adapted from Every Young Man's Battle

For though your hearts were once full of darkness, now
you are full of light from the Lord, and your behavior
should show it! For this light within you produces only
what is good and right and true.

Try to find out what is pleasing to the Lord. Take no
part in the worthless deeds of evil and darkness; instead,
rebuke and expose them.

EPHESIANS 5:8-11, NLT

But let us who live in the light think clearly, protected by
the body armor of faith and love, and wearing as our helmet the confidence of our salvation.

1 THESSALONIANS 5:8, NLT

The night is nearly over; the day is almost here. So let us
put aside the deeds of darkness and put on the armor
of light. Let us behave decently, as in the daytime, not
in orgies and drunkenness, not in sexual immorality
and debauchery, not in dissension and jealousy. Rather,
clothe yourselves with the Lord Jesus Christ, and do
not think about how to gratify the desires of the sinful
nature.

ROMANS 13:12-14, NIV

For you are all children of the light and of the day; we
don't belong to darkness and night. So be on your guard,
not asleep like the others. Stay alert and be sober.

1 THESSALONIANS 5:5-6, NLT

THE COMMAND TO PUT ON THE NEW SELF

You were taught, with regard to your former way of life, to
put off your old self, which is being corrupted by its
deceitful desires; to be made new in the attitude of your
minds; and to put on the new self, created to be like God
in true righteousness and holiness.

EPHESIANS 4:22-24, NIV

Therefore, if anyone is in Christ, he is a new creation; the
old has gone, the new has come!

2 CORINTHIANS 5:17, NIV

Our old sinful selves were crucified with Christ so that sin might lose its power in our lives. We are no longer slaves to sin.

ROMANS 6:6, NLT

THE COMMAND TO LIVE DIFFERENTLY FROM THE WORLD

"Please tell your readers to be leaders," said Cassie. "Help them to set high standards and encourage them to stick to them. Don't make girls constantly have to be the strong ones when temptation hits, because girls don't want to be pressured into doing something they don't really want to do. We want a man we can trust and deeply respect."

—Every Young Man's Battle

Let me say this, then, speaking for the Lord: Live no longer as the unsaved do, for they are blinded and confused. Their closed hearts are full of darkness; they are far away from the life of God because they have shut their minds against him, and they cannot understand his ways. They don't care anymore about right and wrong and have given themselves over to impure ways. They stop at nothing, being driven by their evil minds and reckless lusts.

EPHESIANS 4:17-19, TLB

For you have spent enough time in the past doing what pagans choose to do—living in debauchery, lust,

drunkenness, orgies, carousing and detestable idolatry.
They think it strange that you do not plunge with them
into the same flood of dissipation, and they heap abuse on
you. But they will have to give account to him who is
ready to judge the living and the dead.

1 PETER 4:3-5, NIV

I hate the work of them who turn aside [from the right
path]; it shall not grasp hold of me.

PSALM 101:3, AMP

If anyone loves the world, the love of the Father is not in
him. For everything in the world—the cravings of sinful
man, the lust of his eyes and the boasting of what he has
and does—comes not from the Father but from the world.
The world and its desires pass away, but the man who does
the will of God lives forever.

1 JOHN 2:15-17, NIV

THE COMMAND TO GUARD YOUR HEART AND TO EXHIBIT SELF-CONTROL

For as you know him better, he will give you, through his
great power, everything you need for living a truly good
life: he even shares his own glory and his own goodness
with us! And by that same mighty power he has given us

all the other rich and wonderful blessings he promised; for instance, the promise to save us from the lust and rotten-ness all around us, and to give us his own character.

But to obtain these gifts, you need more than faith; you must also work hard to be good, and even that is not enough. For then you must learn to know God better and discover what he wants you to do. Next, learn to put aside your own desires so that you will become patient and godly, gladly letting God have his way with you. This will make possible the next step, which is for you to enjoy other people and to like them, and finally you will grow to love them deeply. The more you go on in this way, the more you will grow strong spiritually and become fruitful and useful to our Lord Jesus Christ.

2 PETER 1:3-8, TLB

Therefore, prepare your minds for action; be self-controlled; set your hope fully on the grace to be given you when Jesus Christ is revealed.

1 PETER 1:13, NIV

Be self-controlled and alert. Your enemy the devil prowls around like a roaring lion looking for someone to devour. Resist him, standing firm in the faith, because you know that your brothers throughout the world are undergoing the same kind of sufferings.

And the God of all grace, who called you to his eternal glory in Christ, after you have suffered a little while, will himself restore you and make you strong, firm and steadfast. To him be the power for ever and ever. Amen.

1 PETER 5:8-11, NIV

Above all else, guard your heart, for it affects everything you do.

PROVERBS 4:23, NLT

Set your affection on things above, not on things on the earth.

COLOSSIANS 3:2, KJV

A man without self-control
    is like a city broken into and left without walls.

PROVERBS 25:28, RSV

But the fruit of the Spirit is love, joy, peace, patience, kindness, goodness, faithfulness, gentleness, self-control; against such there is no law.

GALATIANS 5:22-23, RSV

The end of all things is near. Therefore be clear minded and self-controlled so that you can pray.

1 PETER 4:7, NIV

And we are instructed to turn from godless living and
sinful pleasures. We should live in this evil world with
self-control, right conduct, and devotion to God, while
we look forward to that wonderful event when the glory
of our great God and Savior, Jesus Christ, will be
revealed.

TITUS 2:12-13, NLT

Now a bishop (superintendent, overseer) must give no
grounds for accusation but must be above reproach, the
husband of one wife, circumspect and temperate and self-
controlled; [he must be] sensible and well behaved and
dignified and lead an orderly (disciplined) life.

1 TIMOTHY 3:2, AMP

For God did not give us a spirit of timidity (of cowardice,
of craven and cringing and fawning fear), but [He has
given us a spirit] of power and of love and of calm and
well-balanced mind and discipline and self-control.

2 TIMOTHY 1:7, AMP

THE COMMAND TO BECOME BLAMELESS

Holiness is not some nebulous thing. It's a series of right choices.
You needn't wait for some holy cloud to form around you. You'll be
holy when you choose not to sin. You're already free from the
power of sexual immorality; you are not yet free from the *habit* of

sexual immorality, until you choose to be—until you say, "That's enough! I'm choosing to live purely!"

—Every Man's Battle

Do everything without complaining or arguing, so that you may become blameless and pure, children of God without fault in a crooked and depraved generation, in which you shine like stars in the universe as you hold out the word of life.

PHILIPPIANS 2:14-16, NIV

So then, dear friends, since you are looking forward to this, make every effort to be found spotless, blameless and at peace with him.

2 PETER 3:14, NIV

For all his laws are constantly before me;
> I have never abandoned his principles.
I am blameless before God;
> I have kept myself from sin.
The LORD rewarded me for doing right,
> because of the innocence of my hands in his
> > sight.
To the faithful you show yourself faithful;
> to those with integrity you show integrity.

PSALM 18:22-25, NLT

Righteousness guards him whose way is blameless.

PROVERBS 13:6, NKJV

I will be careful to lead a blameless life—
when will you come to me?
I will walk in my house
with blameless heart.

PSALM 101:2, NIV

He holds victory in store for the upright,
he is a shield to those whose walk is blameless.

PROVERBS 2:7, NIV

And this I pray, that your love may abound still more and
more in real knowledge and all discernment, so that you
may approve the things that are excellent, in order to be
sincere and blameless until the day of Christ; having been
filled with the fruit of righteousness which comes through
Jesus Christ, to the glory and praise of God.

PHILIPPIANS 1:9-11, NASB

Now may the God of peace Himself sanctify you entirely;
and may your spirit and soul and body be preserved complete, without blame at the coming of our Lord Jesus
Christ.

1 THESSALONIANS 5:23, NASB

In view of this, I also do my best to maintain always a
blameless conscience both before God and before men.

ACTS 24:16, NASB

THE COMMAND TO OBEY

At a single moment, salvation gave us a new life and a new desire
to be sexually pure for the first time. But this new desire alone will
not bring full intimacy with Christ. We must say yes to this new
desire and refuse to ignore it. We must choose oneness and intimacy with Christ. We must choose sexual purity.

—Every Young Man's Battle

Therefore whoever hears these sayings of Mine, and does
them, I will liken him to a wise man who built his house
on the rock: …the floods came, and the winds blew and
beat on that house; and it did not fall.

MATTHEW 7:24,25, NKJV

But if you do not obey the LORD, and if you rebel against
his commands, his hand will be against you, as it was
against your fathers.

1 SAMUEL 12:15, NIV

In God's kingdom, Old Testament or New Testament, choosing obedience has always been central to intimacy with God. Trouble is,

we aren't in search of obedience. We're in search of mere excellence, and His command is *not* enough. We push back, responding, "*Why* should I eliminate every hint? That's too hard!"

We have countless churches filled with countless men encumbered by sexual sin, weakened by low-grade sexual fevers— men happy enough to go to Promise Keepers but too sickly to *be* promise keepers.

A spiritual battle for purity is going on in every heart and soul. The costs are real. Obedience is hard, requiring humility and meekness, very rare elements indeed.

—adapted from Every Man's Battle

Don't you realize that whatever you choose to obey
becomes your master? You can choose sin, which leads to
death, or you can choose to obey God and receive his
approval.

ROMANS 6:16, NLT

Does the LORD delight in burnt offerings and sacrifices
    as much as in obeying the voice of the LORD?
To obey is better than sacrifice,
    and to heed is better than the fat of rams.
For rebellion is like the sin of divination,
    and arrogance like the evil of idolatry.

1 SAMUEL 15:22-23, NIV

This is love for God: to obey his commands. And his commands are not burdensome, for everyone born of God overcomes the world.

1 JOHN 5:3, NIV

the basics of planning for battle

For teens and young adults, sexual gratification comes from three places: the eyes, the mind, and the body. Therefore, as in any war, you must blockade the "shipping lanes" of the eyes and mind that drive you toward sexual sin and that keep your enemy strong. Beyond that, you must also make sure that you have healthy, positive affections and attitudes in your relationships with girls. In other words, you want your heart to be right and your boundaries clear. To accomplish this, you need to build three perimeters of defense into your life:

1. You need to build a line of defense with your *eyes.*
2. You need to build a line of defense in your *mind.*
3. You need to build a line of defense in your *heart.*

Think of the first line of defense—your eyes—as a wall with "Keep Out" signs around it. You defend your eyes by training them to "bounce" from anything sensual.

The second line of defense is your mind. With the mind, you necessarily block out the objects of lust, but you do evaluate and capture them. A key support verse is 2 Corinthians 10:5: "We take captive every thought to make it obedient to Christ" [NIV]. You must train your mind to take thoughts captive, something your mind probably hasn't been inclined to do.

Your third line of defense is your heart. This innermost defense perimeter is built by strengthening the authenticity of your Christian love for the girls you date, as well as increasing your commitment to become a blessing to others. You want to honor and cherish every young woman you date, just as you hope that the guy dating your future wife is honoring and cherishing her.

—*adapted from* **Every Young Man's Battle**

WISE WARRIORS ALWAYS HAVE A PLAN

A wise man is mightier than a strong man, and a man of knowledge is more powerful than a strong man. So don't go to war without wise guidance; victory depends on having many counselors.

PROVERBS 24:5-6, NLT

Prepare plans by consultation,
And make war by wise guidance.

PROVERBS 20:18, NASB

I am warning you ahead of time, dear friends, so that you can watch out and not be carried away by the errors of these wicked people. I don't want you to lose your own secure footing.

2 PETER 3:17, NLT

My child, don't lose sight of good planning and insight. Hang on to them, for they fill you with life and bring you honor and respect. They keep you safe on your way and keep your feet from stumbling.

PROVERBS 3:21-23, NLT

OUR PLANS NEED TO BE IN SYNC WITH GOD'S

Human plans, no matter how wise or well advised, cannot
stand against the LORD.

PROVERBS 21:30, NLT

The one who despises the word will be in debt
    to it,
But the one who fears the commandment will be
    rewarded.

PROVERBS 13:13, NASB

There are many devices in a man's heart; nevertheless the
counsel of the LORD, that shall stand.

PROVERBS 19:21, KJV

No one serving as a soldier gets involved in civilian
affairs—he wants to please his commanding officer.

2 TIMOTHY 2:4, NIV

GOD HAS BIG PLANS FOR THOSE WHO FOLLOW HIS LEAD

"For I know the plans I have for you," declares the LORD,
"plans to prosper you and not to harm you, plans to give
you hope and a future."

JEREMIAH 29:11, NIV

It is God himself who has made us what we are and given us new lives from Christ Jesus; and long ages ago he planned that we should spend these lives in helping others.

EPHESIANS 2:10, TLB

If any one purifies himself from what is ignoble, then he will be a vessel for noble use, consecrated and useful to the master of the house, ready for any good work.

2 TIMOTHY 2:21, RSV

I will let every one who conquers sit beside me on my throne, just as I took my place with my Father on his throne when I had conquered.

REVELATION 3:21, TLB

To him who overcomes and does my will to the end, I will give authority over the nations.

REVELATION 2:26, NIV

I have told you all this so that you may have peace in me. Here on earth you will have many trials and sorrows. But take heart, because I have overcome the world.

JOHN 16:33, NLT

victory can be yours

JESUS SHOWS THAT VICTORY IS POSSIBLE

Jesus' hands never touched a woman with dishonor, but Jesus said that lusting with the eyes is the same as touching. Given that Jesus is sinless, then it is true that Jesus not only never touched a woman with dishonor, He never even *looked* at a woman in dishonor. In this arena, Jesus is clearly our role model.

—*adapted from* Every Man's Battle

Christ, who suffered for you, is your example. Follow in his steps: He never sinned, never told a lie, never answered back when insulted.… He personally carried the load of our sins in his own body when he died on the cross, so that we can be finished with sin and live a good life from now on. For his wounds have healed ours!

1 PETER 2:21-24, TLB

Follow God's example in everything you do, because you are his dear children. Live a life filled with love for others, following the example of Christ, who loved you and gave himself as a sacrifice to take away your sins.

EPHESIANS 5:1-2, NLT

Therefore, when Christ came into the world, he said:…
"Here I am—it is written about me in the scroll—
    I have come to do your will, O God."

HEBREWS 10:5,7, NIV

Since he himself has gone through suffering and temptation, he is able to help us when we are being tempted.

HEBREWS 2:18, NLT

But thanks be to God, which giveth us the victory through
our Lord Jesus Christ.

1 CORINTHIANS 15:57, KJV

JOB SUCCEEDED IN THE BATTLE

His name was Job, a man who exemplifies the essential role
model of sexual purity in Scripture. In the book of the Bible that
tells his story, we see God bragging about Job to Satan: "Have you
considered my servant Job? There is no one on earth like him; he
is blameless and upright, a man who fears God and shuns evil"
(Job 1:8, NIV).

Was God proud of Job? You bet! He applauded His servant's
faithfulness in words of highest praise, and we should seek that
same praise as well.

—*adapted from* Every Man's Battle

There lived in the land of Uz a man named Job—a good
man who feared God and stayed away from evil.

JOB 1:1, TLB

If my heart has been enticed by a woman,
Or if I have lurked at my neighbor's door,

Then let my wife grind for another,

And let others bow down over her.

For that would be wickedness;

Yes, it would be iniquity deserving of judgment.

JOB 31:9-11, NKJV

YOU ARE NOT FIGHTING ALONE

We've known those who have failed in their battle for sexual purity, and we know some who have won. The difference? Those who won hated their impurity. They were going to war and were going to win—or die trying. Every resource was leveled upon the foe.

—Every Man's Battle

But I say, walk and live [habitually] in the [Holy] Spirit [responsive to and controlled and guided by the Spirit]; then you will certainly not gratify the cravings and desires of the flesh (of human nature without God).

GALATIANS 5:16, AMP

Therefore, since we are surrounded by such a great cloud of witnesses, let us throw off everything that hinders and the sin that so easily entangles, and let us run with perseverance the race marked out for us. Let us fix our eyes on Jesus, the author and perfecter of our faith, who for the joy set before him endured the cross, scorning its shame, and sat down at the right hand of the throne of God. Consider him who endured such opposition from sinful men, so that you will not grow weary and lose heart.

HEBREWS 12:1-3, NIV

I pray that your hearts will be flooded with light so that you can understand the wonderful future he has promised to those he called. I want you to realize what a rich and glorious inheritance he has given to his people. I pray that you will begin to understand the incredible greatness of his power for us who believe him. This is the same mighty power that raised Christ from the dead and seated him in the place of honor at God's right hand in the heavenly realms.

EPHESIANS 1:18-20, NLT

I pray that from his glorious, unlimited resources he will give you mighty inner strength through his Holy Spirit.

EPHESIANS 3:16, NLT

you have weapons
at your disposal

It's difficult to be victorious. We tell ourselves repeatedly that we want out, but our words are mere dandelion puffs, blowing about in the weakest breeze. Without resolute manhood girding our words, nothing happens. Following are some action items to help you decisively choose victory in the arena of sexual purity.

—*adapted from* **Every Man's Battle**

PRAYER

When we pray, we aren't praying that He will decide to help us. He has already decided to help us. We are praying so that our hearts will change.

> For what great nation is there who has a god so near to them as the Lord our God is to us in all things for which we call upon Him?
>
> DEUTERONOMY 4:7, AMP

> Be joyful in hope, patient in affliction, faithful in prayer.
>
> ROMANS 12:12, NIV

> Pray then like this:
> Our Father who art in heaven,
> Hallowed be thy name…
> Lead us not into temptation,
>> But deliver us from evil.
>
> MATTHEW 6:9,13, RSV

Garrett, a Bible college sophomore, said, "I used to get lustful thoughts popping up all the time during prayer. But now that my eyes are protected, it doesn't happen, so prayer has become much deeper and uninterrupted."

—*adapted from* Every Young Man's Battle

Be unceasing in prayer [praying perseveringly].

1 THESSALONIANS 5:17, AMP

Don't be weary in prayer; keep at it; watch for God's answers and remember to be thankful when they come.

COLOSSIANS 4:2, TLB

But you, dear friends…pray in the Holy Spirit.

JUDE 20, NIV

Pray all the time. Ask God for anything in line with the Holy Spirit's wishes. Plead with him, reminding him of your needs, and keep praying earnestly for all Christians everywhere.

EPHESIANS 6:18, TLB

WORSHIP

What helps bring true intimacy with God quickly? Worship. We were created to worship. Worship and praise brings intimacy with the Lord and ushers us quickly into His presence.

Chuck Swindoll once mentioned on his *Insight for Living* radio broadcast that he never enters prayer without first entering worship. That's a good place to start. You can memorize a few choruses and hymns and sing them softly to the Lord before beginning prayer.

—adapted from Every Young Man's Battle

Therefore I urge you, brethren, by the mercies of God, to present your bodies a living and holy sacrifice, acceptable to God, which is your spiritual service of worship.

ROMANS 12:1, NASB

Yes, ascribe to the Lord
The glory due his name!
Bring an offering and come before him;
Worship the Lord when clothed with holiness!

1 CHRONICLES 16:29, TLB

Come, let us bow down in worship,
let us kneel before the LORD our Maker.

PSALM 95:6, NIV

Even if you suffer for doing what is right, God will reward you for it. So don't be afraid and don't worry. Instead, you must worship Christ as Lord of your life. And if you are asked about your Christian hope, always be ready to explain it. But you must do this in a gentle and respectful way. Keep your conscience clear. Then if people speak evil against you, they will be ashamed when they see what a good life you live because you belong to Christ. Remember, it is better to suffer for doing good, if that is what God wants, than to suffer for doing wrong!

1 PETER 3:14-17, NLT

You are worthy, O Lord our God,
    to receive glory and honor and power.
For you created everything,
    and it is for your pleasure that they exist and
        were created.

REVELATION 4:11, NLT

YOUR SWORD

You'll need a good Bible verse to use as a sword and rallying point.

Just one? It may be useful to memorize several verses of Scripture about purity since they work to eventually transform and wash the mind. But in the cold-turkey, day-to-day fight against impurity, having several memory verses might be as cumbersome as strapping on a hundred-pound backpack to engage in hand-to-hand combat. That's why we recommend a single "attack verse," and we suggest the opening line of Job 31: "I [have] made a covenant with my eyes" [NIV].

When you fail and look longer than necessary at a hot babe,

sharply say, "No, I've made a covenant with my eyes. I can't do that!" When you're tempted to let your gaze linger on a beautiful woman with a low-cut dress, say, "No, I've made a covenant with my eyes. I can't do that!" This action will be a quick dagger to the heart of your enemy.

—*adapted from* Every Young Man's Battle

And you will need the helmet of salvation and the sword
of the Spirit—which is the Word of God.

EPHESIANS 6:17, TLB

Your word is a lamp to my feet
    and a light for my path.

PSALM 119:105, NIV

Great peace have those who love Your law,
And nothing causes them to stumble.

PSALM 119:165, NKJV

Your words were found, and I ate them; and Your words
were to me a joy and the rejoicing of my heart, for I am
called by Your name, O Lord God of hosts.

JEREMIAH 15:16, AMP

For whatever God says to us is full of living power: it is
sharper than the sharpest dagger, cutting swift and deep

into our innermost thoughts and desires with all their parts, exposing us for what we really are.

HEBREWS 4:12, TLB

YOUR SHIELD

Your shield—a protective verse that you can reflect on and draw strength from even when you aren't in the direct line of fire—may be even more important than your sword because it places temptation out of earshot. We suggest selecting this verse as your shield: "Flee from sexual immorality.... You are not your own; you were bought at a price. Therefore, honor God with your body" (1 Corinthians 6:18-20, NIV).

It also helps to repeat this when facing sensual images or thoughts: "I have no right to look at that or think about it. I haven't the authority."

—adapted from Every Young Man's Battle

In addition to all this, take up the shield of faith, with which you can extinguish all the flaming arrows of the evil one.

EPHESIANS 6:16, NIV

you can't fight this battle alone

While you build real interpersonal intimacy into your life by joining an accountability group, don't forget to place God in the center of the equation. By seeking and asking Him for supernatural help in this battle, you can overcome things that you never thought possible. You'll find yourself hungrier to know Him, and you'll experience a greater desire to communicate with Him. As your intimacy with God grows, you'll need less of that false intimacy. You'll find Him to be your best accountability partner.

—*adapted from* Every Young Man's Battle

WE ARE ACCOUNTABLE TO GOD

What then shall I do when God rises up?
   When he makes inquiry, what shall I answer him?

JOB 31:14, RSV

Arise, O LORD; O God, lift up Your hand.
Do not forget the afflicted.
Why has the wicked spurned God?
He has said to himself, "You will not require it."
You have seen it, for You have beheld mischief and
   vexation to take it into Your hand.
The unfortunate commits himself to You;
You have been the helper of the orphan.
Break the arm of the wicked and the evildoer,
Seek out his wickedness until You find none.

PSALM 10:12-15, NASB

He who deals wisely and heeds [God's] word and counsel shall find good, and whoever leans on, trusts in, and is confident in the Lord—happy, blessed, and fortunate is he.

PROVERBS 16:20, AMP

If you sin without knowing what you're doing, God takes that into account. But if you sin knowing full well what you're doing, that's a different story entirely. Merely hearing God's law is a waste of your time if you don't do what he commands. Doing, not hearing, is what makes the difference with God.

ROMANS 2:12-13, MSG

But I say unto you, That every idle word that men shall speak, they shall give account thereof in the day of judgment.

MATTHEW 12:36, KJV

And he called him, and said unto him, How is it that I hear this of thee? give an account of thy stewardship; for thou mayest be no longer steward.

LUKE 16:2, KJV

For this very reason, Christ died and returned to life so that he might be the Lord of both the dead and the living. You, then, why do you judge your brother? Or why do

you look down on your brother? For we will all stand
before God's judgment seat. It is written:

"'As surely as I live,' says the Lord,

'every knee will bow before me;

every tongue will confess to God.'"

So then, each of us will give an account of himself to God.

ROMANS 14:9-12, NIV

The reverent and worshipful fear of the Lord prolongs
one's days, but the years of the wicked shall be made short.

PROVERBS 10:27, AMP

For God did not call us to be impure, but to live a holy
life. Therefore, he who rejects this instruction does not
reject man but God, who gives you his Holy Spirit.

1 THESSALONIANS 4:7-8, NIV

Nothing in all creation can hide from him. Everything is
naked and exposed before his eyes. This is the God to
whom we must explain all that we have done.

HEBREWS 4:13, NLT

You have had enough in the past of the evil things that
godless people enjoy—their immorality and lust, their
feasting and drunkenness and wild parties, and their
terrible worship of idols.

Of course, your former friends are very surprised when you no longer join them in the wicked things they do, and they say evil things about you. But just remember that they will have to face God, who will judge everyone, both the living and the dead.

1 PETER 4:3-5, NLT

WHEN THE LORD DISCIPLINES YOU

My child, don't ignore it when the LORD disciplines you, and don't be discouraged when he corrects you. For the LORD corrects those he loves, just as a father corrects a child in whom he delights.

PROVERBS 3:11-12, NLT

Behold, happy is the man whom God corrects;
Therefore do not despise the chastening of the Almighty.

JOB 5:17, NKJV

The fear of the LORD is the beginning of knowledge;
Fools despise wisdom and instruction.

PROVERBS 1:7, NASB

Cease listening, my son, to discipline,
And you will stray from the words of knowledge.

PROVERBS 19:27, NASB

Fear of the LORD gives life, security, and protection from harm.

PROVERBS 19:23, NLT

He who keeps instruction is in the way of life,
But he who refuses correction goes astray.

PROVERBS 10:17, NKJV

WE ARE ACCOUNTABLE TO ONE ANOTHER

Many young men fighting for sexual purity seek support in a men's Bible study group or a smaller accountability group with one or two other men. Having a safe place to discuss tough issues often results in honest exchange, although getting there can be awkward.

Honest sharing must occur in these relationships. Tough questions must be asked, and true answers given. Otherwise, you don't have an accountability group at all, but merely a sympathy gathering where each person admits his failure again and again, week after week.

—adapted from Every Young Man's Battle

My eyes will be on the faithful in the land,
    that they may dwell with me;
he whose walk is blameless
    will minister to me.

PSALM 101:6, NIV

It isn't our job to judge outsiders. But it certainly is our job to judge and deal strongly with those who are members of the church, and who are sinning in these ways. God alone is the Judge of those on the outside. But you yourselves must deal with this man and put him out of your church.

1 CORINTHIANS 5:12-13, TLB

Instruct a wise man and he will be wiser still;
    teach a righteous man and he will add to his learning.

PROVERBS 9:9, NIV

A rebuke goes deeper into a man of understanding
    than a hundred blows into a fool.

PROVERBS 17:10, RSV

There are "friends" who destroy each other, but a real friend sticks closer than a brother.

PROVERBS 18:24, NLT

Get all the advice and instruction you can, and be wise the rest of your life.

PROVERBS 19:20, NLT

Open rebuke is better than hidden love!
Wounds from a friend are better than kisses from an
    enemy!

PROVERBS 27:5-6, TLB

Then let us no more criticize and blame and pass judgment on one another, but rather decide and endeavor never to put a stumbling block or an obstacle or a hindrance in the way of a brother.

ROMANS 14:13, AMP

Anyone who loves other Christians is living in the light and does not cause anyone to stumble.

1 JOHN 2:10, NLT

LISTEN TO THOSE WHO HAVE GONE BEFORE YOU

Maybe you aren't concerned with your sexual impurity. Maybe you think that God will forgive you and everything will be over once you marry. He'll forgive you, but it won't be over. Sin comes with inescapable consequences that follow you. You'll have to pay the price at the same toll bridge as the rest of us.

—*adapted from* Every Young Man's Battle

Where there is no guidance the people fall,
But in abundance of counselors there is victory.

PROVERBS 11:14, NASB

Your testimonies also are my delight;
They are my counselors.

PSALM 119:24, NASB

Valid criticism is as treasured by the one who heeds it as jewelry made from finest gold.

PROVERBS 25:12, NLT

Oil and perfume make the heart glad,
So a man's counsel is sweet to his friend.

PROVERBS 27:9, NASB

ACCOUNTABILITY IS VITAL TO YOUR SUCCESS

Without counsel purposes are disappointed; but in the multitude of counsellors they are established.

PROVERBS 15:22, DARBY

The ear that hears the rebukes of life
Will abide among the wise.

PROVERBS 15:31, NKJV

From my experience, I know that fools who turn from God may be successful for the moment, but then comes sudden disaster.

JOB 5:3, NLT

It is safer to meet a bear robbed of her cubs than to confront a fool caught in folly.

PROVERBS 17:12, NLT

rules of engagement

Attraction to the female body is a natural, God-given desire, so it's natural for you to find a girl's beauty tugging at your eyes for attention. You'll be tempted in many wrong ways, however, to play with these natural desires and attractions. Obviously, stripping off her clothes in the basement at the after-game party is a wrong way, but it's just as wrong to stare lustfully at her and fantasize in your mind. Neither practice is any more pure than the other.

—*adapted from* **Every Young Man's Battle**

LEARN TO RECOGNIZE THE SOURCE OF TEMPTATION

Then Jesus was led out into the wilderness by the Holy Spirit to be tempted there by the Devil. For forty days and forty nights he ate nothing and became very hungry. Then the Devil came and said to him, "If you are the Son of God, change these stones into loaves of bread."

MATTHEW 4:1-3, NLT

And remember, when someone wants to do wrong it is never God who is tempting him, for God never wants to do wrong and never tempts anyone else to do it. Temptation is the pull of man's own evil thoughts and wishes. These evil thoughts lead to evil actions and afterwards to the death penalty from God. So don't be misled, dear brothers.

JAMES 1:13-16, TLB

That is why, when I could bear it no longer, I sent Timothy to find out whether your faith was still strong. I was afraid that the Tempter had gotten the best of you and that all our work had been useless.

1 Thessalonians 3:5, NLT

But I am frightened, fearing that in some way you will be led away from your pure and simple devotion to our Lord, just as Eve was deceived by Satan in the Garden of Eden.

2 Corinthians 11:3, TLB

HOW TO DEFEND AGAINST AN ENEMY ATTACK

We use God's mighty weapons, not mere worldly weapons, to knock down the Devil's strongholds. With these weapons we break down every proud argument that keeps people from knowing God.

2 Corinthians 10:4-5, NLT

But remember that the temptations that come into your life are no different from what others experience. And God is faithful. He will keep the temptation from becoming so strong that you can't stand up against it. When you are tempted, he will show you a way out so that you will not give in to it.

1 Corinthians 10:13, NLT

If young toughs tell you, "Come and join us"—turn your back on them!

PROVERBS 1:10, TLB

The name of the LORD is a strong tower;
The righteous run to it and are safe.

PROVERBS 18:10, NKJV

Do not be overcome by evil, but overcome evil with good.

ROMANS 12:21, RSV

Sin is no longer your master, for you are no longer subject to the law, which enslaves you to sin. Instead, you are free by God's grace.

ROMANS 6:14, NLT

When He came to the place, He said to them, "Pray that you may not enter into temptation."

LUKE 22:40, NKJV

HOW TO PREPARE FOR AN ENEMY ATTACK

Watch and pray, lest you enter into temptation. The spirit indeed is willing, but the flesh is weak.

MARK 14:38, NKJV

Brethren, if a man is overtaken in any trespass, you who are spiritual should restore him in a spirit of gentleness. Look to yourself, lest you too be tempted.

GALATIANS 6:1, RSV

Be careful—watch out for attacks from Satan, your great enemy. He prowls around like a hungry, roaring lion, looking for some victim to tear apart. Stand firm when he attacks. Trust the Lord; and remember that other Christians all around the world are going through these sufferings too.

1 PETER 5:8-9, TLB

A final word: Be strong with the Lord's mighty power. Put on all of God's armor so that you will be able to stand firm against all strategies and tricks of the Devil. For we are not fighting against people made of flesh and blood, but against the evil rulers and authorities of the unseen world, against those mighty powers of darkness who rule this world, and against wicked spirits in the heavenly realms.

Use every piece of God's armor to resist the enemy in the time of evil, so that after the battle you will still be standing firm. Stand your ground, putting on the sturdy belt of truth and the body armor of God's righteousness. For shoes, put on the peace that comes from the Good News, so that you will be fully prepared. In every battle you will need faith as your shield to stop the fiery arrows aimed at you by Satan. Put on salvation as your helmet, and take the sword of the Spirit, which is the word of God. Pray at all times and on every occasion in the power of the Holy Spirit. Stay alert and be persistent in your prayers for all Christians everywhere.

EPHESIANS 6:10-18, NLT

Submit yourselves therefore to God. Resist the devil, and he will flee from you.

JAMES 4:7, KJV

when temptation strikes

Your school is likely swarming with girls wearing spaghetti-strap tops, low-cut dresses, and underwear as outerwear. You've got access to X-rated sites on the Internet that weren't there when you were in junior high. When your friends head to the beach or water park, every girl you know sports a bikini.

When you face these different obstacles, it's important to bounce your eyes away, which may sound simple to do, but it isn't. Satan fights you with lies while your body fights you with desires and strength of deeply entrenched bad habits.

—*adapted from* **Every Young Man's Battle**

WHEN YOUR BODY AND MIND TELL YOU TO GO FOR IT

Do not lust after her beauty in your heart,
Nor let her allure you with her eyelids.
For by means of a harlot
A man is reduced to a crust of bread;
And an adulteress will prey upon his precious life.

PROVERBS 6:25-26, NKJV

Be alert and on your guard; stand firm in your faith (your conviction respecting man's relationship to God and divine things, keeping the trust and holy fervor born of faith and a part of it). Act like men and be courageous; grow in strength!

1 CORINTHIANS 16:13, AMP

Let not your heart incline toward her ways, do not stray
into her paths.

PROVERBS 7:25, AMP

A prudent person foresees the danger ahead and takes pre-
cautions. The simpleton goes blindly on and suffers the
consequences.

PROVERBS 27:12, NLT

WHEN SHE ENCOURAGES YOU TO ACT ON YOUR DESIRES

We understand that you are not married yet, so technically speaking, you cannot commit adultery. But the principles in the following verses apply whenever someone engages in sex outside of
marriage:

Whoever commits adultery with a woman lacks
        understanding;
He who does so destroys his own soul.
Wounds and dishonor he will get,
And his reproach will not be wiped away.
For jealousy is a husband's fury;
Therefore he will not spare in the day of vengeance.
He will accept no recompense,
Nor will he be appeased though you give many gifts.

PROVERBS 6:32-35, NKJV

Wisdom will save you from the immoral woman, from the flattery of the adulterous woman. She has abandoned her husband and ignores the covenant she made before God. Entering her house leads to death; it is the road to hell. The man who visits her is doomed. He will never reach the paths of life.

PROVERBS 2:16-19, NLT

For the lips of an immoral woman drip honey,
And her mouth is smoother than oil.

PROVERBS 5:3, NKJV

For these commands are a lamp,
        this teaching is a light,
and the corrections of discipline
        are the way to life,
keeping you from the immoral woman,
        from the smooth tongue of the wayward wife.
Do not lust in your heart after her beauty
        or let her captivate you with her eyes,
for the prostitute reduces you to a loaf of bread,
        and the adulteress preys upon your very life.
Can a man scoop fire into his lap
        without his clothes being burned?
Can a man walk on hot coals
        without his feet being scorched?

So is he who sleeps with another man's wife;

> no one who touches her will go unpunished.

PROVERBS 6:23-29, NIV

For at the window of my house

> I have looked out through my lattice,

and I have seen among the simple,

> I have perceived among the youths,

> a young man without sense,

passing along the street near her corner,

> taking the road to her house

in the twilight, in the evening,

> at the time of night and darkness.

And lo, a woman meets him,

> dressed as a harlot, wily of heart.

She is loud and wayward,

> her feet do not stay at home;

now in the street, now in the market,

> and at every corner she lies in wait.

She seizes him and kisses him,

> and with impudent face she says to him:

"I had to offer sacrifices,

> and today I have paid my vows;

so now I have come out to meet you,

> to seek you eagerly, and I have found you.

"I have decked my couch with coverings,
        colored spreads of Egyptian linen;
I have perfumed my bed with myrrh,
        aloes, and cinnamon.
"Come, let us take our fill of love till morning;
        let us delight ourselves with love.
For my husband is not at home;
        he has gone on a long journey;
he took a bag of money with him;
        at full moon he will come home."

With much seductive speech she persuades him;
        with her smooth talk she compels him.
All at once he follows her,
        as an ox goes to the slaughter,
or as a stag is caught fast
        till an arrow pierces its entrails;
as a bird rushes into a snare;
        he does not know that it will cost him his life.

And now, O sons, listen to me,
        and be attentive to the words of my mouth.
Let not your heart turn aside to her ways,
        do not stray into her paths;
for many a victim has she laid low;
        yea, all her slain are a mighty host.

Her house is the way to Sheol,
> going down to the chambers of death.

PROVERBS 7:6-27, RSV

The mouth of an immoral woman is a deep pit;
He who is abhorred by the LORD will fall there.

PROVERBS 22:14, NKJV

Give me your heart, my son,
And let your eyes delight in my ways.
For a harlot is a deep pit
And an adulterous woman is a narrow well.
Surely she lurks as a robber,
And increases the faithless among men.

PROVERBS 23:26-28, NASB

Why be captivated, my son, with an immoral woman, or embrace the breasts of an adulterous woman? For the LORD sees clearly what a man does.

PROVERBS 5:20,21, NLT

And I discovered more bitter than death the woman whose heart is snares and nets, whose hands are chains. One who is pleasing to God will escape from her, but the sinner will be captured by her.

ECCLESIASTES 7:26, NASB

A man who loves wisdom brings joy to his father,
but a companion of prostitutes squanders his wealth.

PROVERBS 29:3, NIV

WHEN GOD'S PLAN SEEMS TOO STRICT

It is better to spend your time at funerals than at festivals.
For you are going to die, and you should think about it
while there is still time.

ECCLESIASTES 7:2, NLT

Be careful! Watch out for attacks from the Devil, your
great enemy. He prowls around like a roaring lion, looking
for some victim to devour. Take a firm stand against him,
and be strong in your faith. Remember that your Christian
brothers and sisters all over the world are going through
the same kind of suffering you are.

In his kindness God called you to his eternal glory by
means of Jesus Christ. After you have suffered a little
while, he will restore, support, and strengthen you, and he
will place you on a firm foundation. All power is his forever and ever. Amen.

1 PETER 5:8-11, NLT

For man does not know his time. Like fish which are taken
in an evil net, and like birds which are caught in a snare, so

the sons of men are snared at an evil time, when it suddenly falls upon them.

ECCLESIASTES 9:12, RSV

Man cannot abide in his pomp,
> he is like the beasts that perish.

PSALM 49:12, RSV

JESUS REVEALS THE PATH OF VICTORY

Pray like this:
Our Father in heaven,
> may your name be honored.

May your Kingdom come soon.
May your will be done here on earth,
> just as it is in heaven.

Give us our food for today,
and forgive us our sins,
> just as we have forgiven those who have sinned
> > against us.

And don't let us yield to temptation,
> but deliver us from the evil one.

MATTHEW 6:9-13, NLT

They went to a place called Gethsemane, and Jesus said to his disciples, "Sit here while I pray." He took Peter, James and John along with him, and he began to be deeply distressed and troubled. "My soul is overwhelmed with sorrow to the point of death," he said to them. "Stay here and keep watch."

Going a little farther, he fell to the ground and prayed that if possible the hour might pass from him. "Abba, Father," he said, "everything is possible for you. Take this cup from me. Yet not what I will, but what you will."

Then he returned to his disciples and found them sleeping. "Simon," he said to Peter, "are you asleep? Could you not keep watch for one hour? Watch and pray so that you will not fall into temptation. The spirit is willing, but the body is weak."

MARK 14:32-38, NIV

Then Jesus, full of the Holy Spirit, left the Jordan River, being urged by the Spirit out into the barren wastelands of Judea, where Satan tempted him for forty days. He ate nothing all that time, and was very hungry.

Satan said, "If you are God's Son, tell this stone to become a loaf of bread."

But Jesus replied, "It is written in the Scriptures, 'Other things in life are much more important than bread!'"

Then Satan took him up and revealed to him all the kingdoms of the world in a moment of time; and the devil told him, "I will give you all these splendid kingdoms and their glory—for they are mine to give to anyone I wish—if you will only get down on your knees and worship me."

Jesus replied, "We must worship God, and him alone. So it is written in the Scriptures."

Then Satan took him to Jerusalem to a high roof of the Temple and said, "If you are the Son of God, jump off! For the Scriptures say that God will send his angels to guard you and to keep you from crashing to the pavement below!"

Jesus replied, "The Scriptures also say, 'Do not put the Lord your God to a foolish test.'"

When the devil had ended all the temptations, he left Jesus for a while and went away.

Then Jesus returned to Galilee, full of the Holy Spirit's power.

LUKE 4:1-14, TLB

This High Priest of ours understands our weaknesses, for he faced all of the same temptations we do, yet he did not sin.

HEBREWS 4:15, NLT

Therefore, since the children share in flesh and blood, He Himself likewise also partook of the same, that through death He might render powerless him who had the power of death, that is, the devil, and might free those who through fear of death were subject to slavery all their lives. For assuredly He does not give help to angels, but He gives help to the descendant of Abraham. Therefore, He had to be made like His brethren in all things, so that He might become a merciful and faithful high priest in things pertaining to God, to make propitiation for the sins of the people. For since He Himself was tempted in that which He has suffered, He is able to come to the aid of those who are tempted.

HEBREWS 2:14-18, NASB

what the enemy
doesn't want you to know

THE DEVASTATING CONSEQUENCES OF SIN

Fred Stoeker says: "I finally made the connection between my sexual immorality and my distance from God. Having eliminated the visible adulteries and pornography, and having avoided physical adultery, I looked pure on the outside to everyone else. But to God, I had stopped short, and I'd ignored His voice repeatedly as He prodded me in these areas. I'd merely found a comfortable middle ground somewhere between paganism and obedience to God's standard. God desired more for me."

—*adapted from* **Every Young Man's Battle**

He who troubles his own house shall inherit the wind, and the foolish shall be servant to the wise of heart.

PROVERBS 11:29, AMP

If the righteous will be rewarded in the earth,
How much more the wicked and the sinner!

PROVERBS 11:31, NASB

Adversity pursues sinners,
But the righteous will be rewarded with prosperity.

PROVERBS 13:21, NASB

And if it is with difficulty that the righteous is saved, what will become of the godless man and the sinner?

1 PETER 4:18, NASB

Will those who do evil never learn?…
Terror will grip them,
> for God is with those who obey him.

PSALM 14:4-5, NLT

I show this unfailing love to many thousands by forgiving every kind of sin and rebellion. Even so I do not leave sin unpunished, but I punish the children for the sins of their parents to the third and fourth generations.

EXODUS 34:7, NLT

If also after these things you do not obey Me, then I will punish you seven times more for your sins.

LEVITICUS 26:18, NASB

WHAT HAPPENS TO SOLDIERS WHO SURRENDER TO THE ENEMY

Their future is eternal destruction. Their god is their appetite, they brag about shameful things, and all they think about is this life here on earth.

PHILIPPIANS 3:19, NLT

So God let them go ahead and do whatever shameful things their hearts desired. As a result, they did vile and degrading things with each other's bodies…. And the men, instead of having normal sexual relationships with women, burned with lust for each other. Men did shameful things with other men and, as a result, suffered within themselves the penalty they so richly deserved.

ROMANS 1:24,27, NLT

One day Dinah, Leah's daughter, went to visit some of the young women who lived in the area. But when the local prince, Shechem son of Hamor the Hivite, saw her, he took her and raped her…. Word soon reached Jacob that his daughter had been defiled, but his sons were out in the fields herding cattle so he did nothing until they returned…. He [Shechem's father] arrived just as Jacob's sons were coming in from the fields. They were shocked and furious that their sister had been raped. Shechem had done a disgraceful thing against Jacob's family, a thing that should never have been done.

But three days later…two of Dinah's brothers, Simeon and Levi, took their swords, entered the town without opposition, and slaughtered every man there, including Hamor and Shechem. They rescued Dinah from Shechem's house and returned to their camp. Then all of Jacob's sons plundered the town because their sister had been defiled there. They seized all the flocks and herds and donkeys—everything they could lay their hands on, both inside the town and outside in the fields.

GENESIS 34:1-2,5,7,25-28, NLT

In a similar way, Sodom and Gomorrah and the surrounding towns gave themselves up to sexual immorality and perversion. They serve as an example of those who suffer the punishment of eternal fire.

JUDE 7, NIV

Keep to a path far from her,
    do not go near the door of her house,
lest you give your best strength to others
    and your years to one who is cruel,
lest strangers feast on your wealth
    and your toil enrich another man's house.
At the end of your life you will groan,
    when your flesh and body are spent.
You will say, "How I hated discipline!
    How my heart spurned correction!
I would not obey my teachers
    or listen to my instructors.
I have come to the brink of utter ruin
    in the midst of the whole assembly."

PROVERBS 5:8-14, NIV

Each one is tempted when, by his own evil desire, he is dragged away and enticed. Then, after desire has conceived, it gives birth to sin; and sin…gives birth to death.

JAMES 1:14-15, NIV

GOD WON'T TOLERATE COMPROMISE—
AND NEITHER SHOULD YOU

When we call ourselves Christians but don't act like it, Jesus force-fully objects. Luke 6:46 says, "Why do you call me, 'Lord, Lord,' and do not do what I say?" (NIV).

—*adapted from* Every Young Man's Battle

And he answered and said unto them, Have ye not read, that he which made them at the beginning made them male and female, and said, For this cause shall a man leave father and mother, and shall cleave to his wife: and they twain shall be one flesh? Wherefore they are no more twain, but one flesh. What therefore God hath joined together, let not man put asunder.

MATTHEW 19:4-6, KJV

Do not yield your members to sin as instruments of wickedness, but yield yourselves to God as men who have been brought from death to life, and your members to God as instruments of righteousness.

ROMANS 6:13, RSV

Therefore, I urge you, brothers, in view of God's mercy, to offer your bodies as living sacrifices, holy and pleasing to God—this is your spiritual act of worship. Do not con-form any longer to the pattern of this world, but be transformed by the renewing of your mind. Then you will be able to test and approve what God's will is—his good, pleasing and perfect will.

ROMANS 12:1-2, NIV

When I [Paul] wrote to you before, I told you not to associate with people who indulge in sexual sin.

1 CORINTHIANS 5:9, NLT

So put to death the sinful, earthly things lurking within you. Have nothing to do with sexual sin, impurity, lust, and shameful desires.

COLOSSIANS 3:5, NLT

Do you not know that your bodies are members of Christ? Shall I therefore take the members of Christ and make them members of a prostitute? Never! Do you not know that he who joins himself to a prostitute becomes one body with her? For, as it is written, "The two shall become one." But he who is united to the Lord becomes one spirit with him. Shun immorality. Every other sin which a man commits is outside the body; but the immoral man sins against his own body. Do you not know that your body is a temple of the Holy Spirit within you, which you have from God? You are not your own; you were bought with a price. So glorify God in your body.

1 CORINTHIANS 6:15-20, RSV

A REVEALING LOOK AT THE ENEMY'S TACTICS

I was looking out the window of my house one day and saw a simpleminded young man who lacked common sense. He was crossing the street near the house of an immoral woman. He was strolling down the path by her house at twilight, as the day was fading, as the dark of night set in. The woman approached him, dressed seductively and sly of heart. She was the brash, rebellious type who never stays at home. She is often seen in the streets and markets, soliciting at every corner.

She threw her arms around him and kissed him, and with a brazen look she said, "I've offered my sacrifices and just finished my vows. It's you I was looking for! I came out to find you, and here you are! My bed is spread with colored sheets of finest linen imported from Egypt. I've perfumed my bed with myrrh, aloes, and cinnamon. Come, let's drink our fill of love until morning. Let's enjoy each other's caresses, for my husband is not home. He's away on a long trip. He has taken a wallet full of money with him, and he won't return until later in the month."

So she seduced him with her pretty speech. With her flattery she enticed him. He followed her at once, like an ox going to the slaughter or like a trapped stag, awaiting the arrow that would pierce its heart. He was like a bird flying into a snare, little knowing it would cost him his life.

PROVERBS 7:6-23, NLT

**pride sets you up for a fall,
so don't stop short**

Knowing that God's standard is the standard of true life, Josiah rose up and tore down *everything* that was in opposition to God. And what about you? Now that you've heard about God's standard of sexual purity, are you willing, in the spirit of Josiah, to make a covenant to hold to that standard with all your heart and soul? Will you tear down every sexual thing that stands in opposition to God?

Can you see that you've been living the mixed standards of mere excellence? Stopping short but still looking Christian enough?

Or have you aimed for obedience and perfection, where you're truly called to go?

—**Every Man's Battle**

BROKENNESS COMES WITH PRIDE

Haughty eyes and a proud heart,
    the lamp of the wicked, are sin.

PROVERBS 21:4, RSV

For many walk, of whom I have told you often, and now
tell you even weeping, that they are the enemies of the
cross of Christ: whose end is destruction, whose god is
their belly, and whose glory is in their shame—who set
their mind on earthly things.

PHILIPPIANS 3:18-19, NKJV

Haughtiness goes before destruction; humility precedes
honor.

PROVERBS 18:12, NLT

Pride goes before destruction,
and a haughty spirit before a fall.
It is better to be of a lowly spirit with the poor
than to divide the spoil with the proud.

PROVERBS 16:18,19 RSV

Enter through the narrow gate; for wide is the gate and
spacious and broad is the way that leads away to destruction, and many are those who are entering through it.

MATTHEW 7:13, AMP

But there were also false prophets among the people, just
as there will be false teachers among you. They will secretly
introduce destructive heresies, even denying the sovereign
Lord who bought them—bringing swift destruction on
themselves.

2 PETER 2:1, NIV

Though you already know all this, I want to remind you
that the Lord delivered his people out of Egypt, but later
destroyed those who did not believe.

JUDE 5, NIV

WHAT PRIDE WILL DO TO YOU

But when [Uzziah] became strong, his heart was so proud that he acted corruptly, and he was unfaithful to the LORD his God.… And while he was enraged with the priests, the leprosy broke out on his forehead…because the LORD had smitten him. King Uzziah was a leper to the day of his death.

2 CHRONICLES 26:16,19,20-21, NASB

The LORD despises pride; be assured that the proud will be punished.

PROVERBS 16:5, NLT

The Lord hates the stubborn but delights in those who are good.

You can be very sure that the evil man will not go unpunished forever. And you can also be very sure that God will rescue the children of the godly.

PROVERBS 11:20-21, TLB

Better it is to be of an humble spirit with the lowly, than to divide the spoil with the proud.

PROVERBS 16:19, KJV

The LORD mocks at mockers, but he shows favor to the humble.

PROVERBS 3:34, NLT

DISCOVER THE POWER OF HUMILITY

By humility and the fear of the LORD are riches, and honour, and life.

PROVERBS 22:4, KJV

When pride comes, then comes dishonor,
But with the humble is wisdom.

PROVERBS 11:2, NASB

My hand has made both earth and skies, and they are mine. Yet I will look with pity on the man who has a humble and a contrite heart, who trembles at my word.

ISAIAH 66:2, TLB

A man's pride will bring him low,
But a humble spirit will obtain honor.

PROVERBS 29:23, NASB

For whoever exalts himself will be humbled, and he who humbles himself will be exalted.

LUKE 14:11, NKJV

But the humble will inherit the land
And will delight themselves in abundant prosperity.

PSALM 37:11, NASB

Fear of the LORD teaches a person to be wise; humility precedes honor.

PROVERBS 15:33, NLT

Humble yourselves in the sight of the Lord, and he shall lift you up.

JAMES 4:10, KJV

when you've fallen into sin

FACING THE GRAVITY OF YOUR SIN

O my God, I am too ashamed and disgraced to lift up my face to you, my God, because our sins are higher than our heads and our guilt has reached to the heavens.

Ezra 9:6, niv

O loving and kind God, have mercy. Have pity upon me and take away the awful stain of my transgressions. Oh, wash me, cleanse me from this guilt. Let me be pure again. For I admit my shameful deed—it haunts me day and night. It is against you and you alone I sinned, and did this terrible thing. You saw it all, and your sentence against me is just. But I was born a sinner, yes, from the moment my mother conceived me. You deserve honesty from the heart; yes, utter sincerity and truthfulness. Oh, give me this wisdom.

Sprinkle me with the cleansing blood and I shall be clean again. Wash me and I shall be whiter than snow. And after you have punished me, give me back my joy again. Don't keep looking at my sins—erase them from your sight. Create in me a new, clean heart, O God, filled with clean thoughts and right desires. Don't toss me aside, banished forever from your presence. Don't take your Holy Spirit from me. Restore to me again the joy of your salvation, and make me willing to obey you.

Psalm 51:1-12, tlb

If we say that we have no sin, we are deceiving ourselves and the truth is not in us. If we confess our sins, He is faithful and righteous to forgive us our sins and to cleanse us from all unrighteousness. If we say that we have not sinned, we make Him a liar and His word is not in us.

1 JOHN 1:8-10, NASB

God doesn't listen to the prayers of men who flout the law.

PROVERBS 28:9, TLB

For whoever keeps the whole law and yet stumbles in one point, he has become guilty of all. For He who said, "Do not commit adultery," also said, "Do not commit murder." Now if you do not commit adultery, but do commit murder, you have become a transgressor of the law.

JAMES 2:10-11, NASB

YOU DON'T HAVE TO BE A SLAVE TO SIN

The Spirit of the Lord is upon me,
because he has anointed me to preach good news
    to the poor.
He has sent me to proclaim release to the captives
and recovering of sight to the blind,
to set at liberty those who are oppressed,
to proclaim the acceptable year of the Lord.

LUKE 4:18-19, RSV

Jesus said to the people who believed in him, "You are truly my disciples if you keep obeying my teachings. And you will know the truth, and the truth will set you free."

"But we are descendants of Abraham," they said. "We have never been slaves to anyone on earth. What do you mean, 'set free'?"

Jesus replied, "I assure you that everyone who sins is a slave of sin. A slave is not a permanent member of the family, but a son is part of the family forever. So if the Son sets you free, you will indeed be free."

JOHN 8:31-36, NLT

Knowing this, that our old self was crucified with Him, in order that our body of sin might be done away with, so that we would no longer be slaves to sin; for he who has died is freed from sin.

ROMANS 6:6-7, NASB

Now the Lord is the Spirit; and where the Spirit of the Lord is, there is liberty.

2 CORINTHIANS 3:17, NKJV

Stand fast therefore in the liberty by which Christ has made us free, and do not be entangled again with a yoke of bondage.

GALATIANS 5:1, NKJV

This righteousness from God comes through faith in Jesus Christ to all who believe. There is no difference, for all have sinned and fall short of the glory of God, and are justified freely by his grace through the redemption that came by Christ Jesus.

ROMANS 3:22-24, NIV

But the Scripture has shut up everyone under sin, so that the promise by faith in Jesus Christ might be given to those who believe.

GALATIANS 3:22, NASB

And do not enter into judgment with Your servant, For in Your sight no man living is righteous.

PSALM 143:2, NASB

That is why he is the one who mediates the new covenant between God and people, so that all who are invited can receive the eternal inheritance God has promised them. For Christ died to set them free from the penalty of the sins they had committed under that first covenant.

HEBREWS 9:15, NLT

FORGIVENESS IS JUST A PRAYER AWAY

If we say that we have no sin, we are deceiving ourselves and the truth is not in us. If we confess our sins, He is faithful and righteous to forgive us our sins and to cleanse us from all unrighteousness. If we say that we have not sinned, we make Him a liar and His word is not in us.

1 JOHN 1:8-10, NASB

Answer me when I call, O God of my righteousness!
You have relieved me in my distress;
Be gracious to me and hear my prayer.

PSALM 4:1, NASB

For this is what the high and lofty One says—
    he who lives forever, whose name is holy:
"I live in a high and holy place,
    but also with him who is contrite and lowly in spirit,
to revive the spirit of the lowly
    and to revive the heart of the contrite.
I will not accuse forever,
    nor will I always be angry,
for then the spirit of man would grow faint before me—
    the breath of man that I have created."

ISAIAH 57:15-16, NIV

But He, being full of compassion, forgave their iniquity,
And did not destroy them.
Yes, many a time He turned His anger away,
And did not stir up all His wrath.

PSALM 78:38, NKJV

Come, let us return to the LORD;
> for he has torn, that he may heal us;
> he has stricken, and he will bind us up.
After two days he will revive us;
> on the third day he will raise us up,
> that we may live before him.
Let us know, let us press on to know the LORD;
> his going forth is sure as the dawn;
he will come to us as the showers,
> as the spring rains that water the earth.

HOSEA 6:1-3, RSV

Finally, I confessed all my sins to you
> and stopped trying to hide them.
I said to myself, "I will confess my rebellion to the LORD."

PSALM 32:5, NLT

A man who refuses to admit his mistakes can never be successful. But if he confesses and forsakes them, he gets another chance.

PROVERBS 28:13, TLB

GOD IS EAGER TO GIVE YOU A FRESH START

As far as the east is from the west,
So far has He removed our transgressions from us.

PSALM 103:12, NASB

Let the wicked forsake his way,
And the unrighteous man his thoughts;
Let him return to the LORD,
And He will have mercy on him;
And to our God,
For He will abundantly pardon.

ISAIAH 55:7, NKJV

Then David said to Nathan, "I have sinned against the
LORD." And Nathan said to David, "The LORD also has
taken away your sin; you shall not die."

2 SAMUEL 12:13, NASB

Yes, it was good for me to suffer this anguish,
     for you have rescued me from death
     and have forgiven all my sins.

ISAIAH 38:17, NLT

For behold, upon the stone which I have set before Joshua,
upon a single stone with seven facets, I will engrave its
inscription, says the LORD of hosts, and I will remove the
guilt of this land in a single day.

ZECHARIAH 3:9, RSV

"But this is the new covenant I will make with the people
of Israel on that day," says the LORD. "I will put my laws in

their minds, and I will write them on their hearts. I will be their God, and they will be my people. And they will not need to teach their neighbors, nor will they need to teach their family, saying, 'You should know the LORD.' For everyone, from the least to the greatest, will already know me," says the LORD. "And I will forgive their wickedness and will never again remember their sins."

JEREMIAH 31:33-34, NLT

If that had been necessary, he would have had to die again and again, ever since the world began. But no! He came once for all time, at the end of the age, to remove the power of sin forever by his sacrificial death for us.

HEBREWS 9:26, NLT

For I will be merciful and gracious toward their sins and I will remember their deeds of unrighteousness no more.

HEBREWS 8:12, AMP

WHEN YOU THINK GOD IS ANGRY WITH YOU

He passed in front of Moses and said, "I am the LORD, I am the LORD, the merciful and gracious God. I am slow to anger and rich in unfailing love and faithfulness."

EXODUS 34:6, NLT

The LORD is slow to anger and abundant in lovingkindness, forgiving iniquity and transgression.

NUMBERS 14:18, NASB

For the LORD your God is a compassionate God; He will not fail you nor destroy you nor forget the covenant with your fathers which He swore to them.

DEUTERONOMY 4:31, NASB

For His anger is but for a moment,
His favor is for life;
Weeping may endure for a night,
But joy comes in the morning.

PSALM 30:5, NKJV

But You, O Lord, are a God merciful and gracious,
Slow to anger and abundant in lovingkindness and truth.

PSALM 86:15, NASB

The LORD is compassionate and gracious,
Slow to anger and abounding in lovingkindness.
He will not always strive with us,
Nor will He keep His anger forever.
He has not dealt with us according to our sins,
Nor rewarded us according to our iniquities.
For as high as the heavens are above the earth,
So great is His lovingkindness toward those who fear Him.

As far as the east is from the west,
So far has He removed our transgressions from us.
Just as a father has compassion on his children,
So the LORD has compassion on those who fear Him.
For He Himself knows our frame;
He is mindful that we are but dust.

PSALM 103:8-14, NASB

The LORD is kind and merciful,
    slow to get angry, full of unfailing love.

PSALM 145:8, NLT

They refused to listen,
And did not remember Your wondrous deeds which You
        had performed among them;
So they became stubborn and appointed a leader to return
        to their slavery in Egypt.
But You are a God of forgiveness,
Gracious and compassionate,
Slow to anger and abounding in lovingkindness;
And You did not forsake them.

NEHEMIAH 9:17, NASB

For I [know] you [are] a gracious God, merciful, slow to
get angry, and full of kindness; I [know] how easily you
could cancel your plans for destroying these people.

JONAH 4:2, TLB

This righteousness from God comes through faith in Jesus Christ to all who believe. There is no difference, for all have sinned and fall short of the glory of God, and are justified freely by his grace through the redemption that came by Christ Jesus.

ROMANS 3:22-24, NIV

And God has actually given us his Spirit (not the world's spirit) so we can know the wonderful things God has freely given us.

1 CORINTHIANS 2:12, NLT

Long ago, even before he made the world, God loved us and chose us in Christ to be holy and without fault in his eyes. His unchanging plan has always been to adopt us into his own family by bringing us to himself through Jesus Christ. And this gave him great pleasure.

So we praise God for the wonderful kindness he has poured out on us because we belong to his dearly loved Son.

EPHESIANS 1:4-6, NLT

WHEN YOU THINK YOU'RE BEYOND HELP

Before we experience victory over sexual sin, we're hurting and confused. *Why can't I win at this?* we think. As the fight wears on, and the losses pile higher, we begin to doubt everything about ourselves, even our salvation. At best, we think that we're deeply flawed, or worse, evil persons.

—Every Young Man's Battle

Let, I pray thee, thy merciful kindness be for my comfort, according to thy word unto thy servant.

PSALM 119:76, KJV

For you were straying like sheep, but have now returned to the Shepherd and Guardian of your souls.

1 PETER 2:25, RSV

I will search for my lost ones who strayed away, and I will bring them safely home again. I will bind up the injured and strengthen the weak. But I will destroy those who are fat and powerful. I will feed them, yes—feed them justice!

EZEKIEL 34:16, NLT

Once you were alienated from God and were enemies in your minds because of your evil behavior. But now he has reconciled you by Christ's physical body through death to present you holy in his sight, without blemish and free from accusation.

COLOSSIANS 1:21-22, NIV

Once we, too, were foolish and disobedient. We were misled by others and became slaves to many wicked desires and evil pleasures. Our lives were full of evil and envy. We hated others, and they hated us.

But then God our Savior showed us his kindness and love. He saved us, not because of the good things we did, but because of his mercy. He washed away our sins and gave us a new life through the Holy Spirit. He generously poured out the Spirit upon us because of what Jesus Christ our Savior did. He declared us not guilty because of his great kindness. And now we know that we will inherit eternal life.

TITUS 3:3-7, NLT

Rejoice always, pray constantly, give thanks in all circumstances; for this is the will of God in Christ Jesus for you.

1 THESSALONIANS 5:16-18, RSV

God's work and commitment on your behalf

Each one of us has been manipulated by our sexual culture; each of us has made choices to sin. To varying degrees, each of us became ensnared by these choices, but we can overcome this affliction. Far too often, however, we ignore our own responsibility in this. We complain, "Well, of course I want to be free from impurity! I've been to the altar 433 times about it, haven't I? It just doesn't seem to be God's will to free me."

Not God's will? That's an offense to the character of God. Don't blame God.

God's will is for you to have sexual purity, though you may not think so since this hasn't been your constant experience. But He *has* made a provision for that purity.

—**Every Man's Battle**

GOD CLEARLY EXPRESSES HIS WILL FOR YOU

It is God's will that you should be sanctified: that you should avoid sexual immorality, that each of you should learn to control his own body in a way that is holy and honorable.

1 THESSALONIANS 4:3-4, NIV

But be holy now in everything you do, just as the Lord is holy, who invited you to be his child. He himself has said, "You must be holy, for I am holy."

1 PETER 1:15, TLB

GOD IS WORKING TO TEACH YOU

For the grace of God that brings salvation has appeared to all men. It teaches us to say "No" to ungodliness and worldly passions, and to live self-controlled, upright and godly lives in this present age, while we wait for the blessed hope—the glorious appearing of our great God and Savior, Jesus Christ.

TITUS 2:11-13, NIV

I will praise the LORD, who counsels me;
    even at night my heart instructs me.

PSALM 16:7, NIV

Good and upright is the LORD;
Therefore He instructs sinners in the way.
He leads the humble in justice,
And He teaches the humble His way.
He will instruct him in the way he should choose.

PSALM 25:8-9,12, NASB

But when the Father sends the Counselor as my representative—and by the Counselor I mean the Holy Spirit—he will teach you everything and will remind you of everything I myself have told you.

JOHN 14:26, NLT

GOD WANTS TO ENCOURAGE YOU

And the work of righteousness will be peace,
And the service of righteousness, quietness and confidence
     forever.

ISAIAH 32:17, NASB

Surely he will never be shaken;
     a righteous man will be remembered forever.
He will have no fear of bad news;
     his heart is steadfast, trusting in the LORD.
His heart is secure, he will have no fear;
     in the end he will look in triumph on his foes.

PSALM 112:6-8, NIV

You have made known to me the path of life;
     you will fill me with joy in your presence,
     with eternal pleasures at your right hand.

PSALM 16:11, NIV

Give your burdens to the LORD.
     and he will take care of you.

PSALM 55:22, NLT

For I the LORD thy God will hold thy right hand, saying
unto thee, Fear not; I will help thee.

ISAIAH 41:13, KJV

GOD HAS PROMISED TO WALK WITH YOU

God's help for you in this battle is sure. God sent His son to brutally die so that you might gain the freedom to say no to sin. He placed the new life of Christ in you to transform you. He sent His Spirit to comfort and guide you.

—Every Young Man's Battle

And surely I am with you always, to the very end of the age.

MATTHEW 28:20, NIV

When you pass through the waters, I will be with you;
And through the rivers, they will not overflow you.
When you walk through the fire, you will not be scorched,
Nor will the flame burn you.

ISAIAH 43:2, NASB

Don't be afraid, for the Lord will go before you and will be with you; he will not fail nor forsake you.

DEUTERONOMY 31:8, TLB

GOD IS WORKING TO SANCTIFY YOU

May the God of peace himself make you entirely pure and devoted to God; and may your spirit and soul and body be kept strong and blameless until that day when our Lord Jesus Christ comes back again. God, who called you to become his child, will do all this for you, just as he promised.

1 THESSALONIANS 5:23-24, TLB

"Come now, let us argue this out," says the LORD. "No matter how deep the stain of your sins, I can remove it. I can make you as clean as freshly fallen snow. Even if you are stained as red as crimson, I can make you as white as wool."

ISAIAH 1:18, NLT

But if we walk in the light as He is in the light, we have fellowship with one another, and the blood of Jesus Christ His Son cleanses us from all sin.

1 JOHN 1:7, NKJV

And so we keep on praying for you that our God will make you the kind of children he wants to have—will make you as good as you wish you could be!—rewarding your faith with his power.

2 THESSALONIANS 1:11, TLB

And I am sure that God who began the good work within you will keep right on helping you grow in his grace until his task within you is finally finished on that day when Jesus Christ returns.

PHILIPPIANS 1:6, TLB

GOD HAS PROMISED TO STRENGTHEN YOU

God is waiting for you. But He is not waiting by the altar, hoping you'll drop by and talk for a while. He is waiting for you to rise up and engage in the battle.

—Every Man's Battle

So do not fear, for I am with you;
   do not be dismayed, for I am your God.
I will strengthen you and help you;
   I will uphold you with my righteous right hand.

ISAIAH 41:10, NIV

Revive us, and we will call upon Your name.

PSALM 80:18, NASB

As a result, Christ will make your hearts strong, blameless, and holy when you stand before God our Father on that day when our Lord Jesus comes with all those who belong to him.

1 THESSALONIANS 3:13, NLT

Each time he said, "My gracious favor is all you need. My power works best in your weakness." So now I am glad to boast about my weaknesses, so that the power of Christ may work through me.

2 CORINTHIANS 12:9, NLT

GOD'S WORD IS AVAILABLE TO WORK IN YOU

Garrett exclaimed, "You wouldn't believe it! I'd been in ministerial studies for a year and a half already, so you have to know that I was reading my Bible plenty. But when I started bouncing my eyes, and the lust rolled away, it was as if the Bible opened up like a blue sky before me after a really dark night. Bouncing my eyes really helped me read my Bible better.

"And I've noticed an interesting thing: When I read my Bible less and don't stay close to the Word, it's harder to bounce my eyes. They really go hand in hand, and one can't be done very well without the other."

—*adapted from* Every Young Man's Battle

And we will never stop thanking God for this: that when we preached to you, you didn't think of the words we spoke as being just our own, but you accepted what we said as the very Word of God—which, of course, it was—and it changed your lives when you believed it.

1 THESSALONIANS 2:13, TLB

For the word of God is living and active. Sharper than any double-edged sword, it penetrates even to dividing soul and spirit, joints and marrow; it judges the thoughts and attitudes of the heart.

HEBREWS 4:12, NIV

How can a young man cleanse his way?
By taking heed according to Your word.

PSALM 119:9, NKJV

The whole Bible was given to us by inspiration from God and is useful to teach us what is true and to make us realize what is wrong in our lives; it straightens us out and helps us do what is right. It is God's way of making us well prepared at every point, fully equipped to do good to everyone.

2 TIMOTHY 3:16-17, TLB

Blessed are all who hear the Word of God and put it into practice.

LUKE 11:28, TLB

GOD IS COMMITTED TO MAKING YOU HOLY

Our fathers disciplined us for a little while as they thought best; but God disciplines us for our good, that we may share in his holiness. No discipline seems pleasant at the time, but painful. Later on, however, it produces a harvest of righteousness and peace for those who have been trained by it.

HEBREWS 12:10-11, NIV

I continually discipline and punish everyone I love;
so I must punish you, unless you turn from your

indifference and become enthusiastic about the things of God.

REVELATION 3:19, TLB

And have you quite forgotten the encouraging words God spoke to you, his child? He said, "My son, don't be angry when the Lord punishes you. Don't be discouraged when he has to show you where you are wrong. For when he punishes you, it proves that he loves you. When he whips you it proves you are really his child."

HEBREWS 12:5-6, TLB

GOD IS LISTENING TO JESUS, OUR ADVOCATE

Who is he who condemns? It is Christ who died, and furthermore is also risen, who is even at the right hand of God, who also makes intercession for us.

ROMANS 8:34, NKJV

Therefore he is able to save completely those who come to God through him, because he always lives to intercede for them.

HEBREWS 7:25, NIV

My little children… If anyone sins, we have an Advocate with the Father, Jesus Christ the righteous.

1 JOHN 2:1, NASB

a battle plan for
the eyes and mind

For most young men, the eyes bounce *toward* the sexual and not *away* from it. To combat years and years of this reflexive action, you need to train your eyes to immediately bounce away when they come upon a sexy image—much like the way you jerk your hand away from a hot stove. Here is what you want to do in a nutshell: When your eyes bounce toward a woman's attributes, they must bounce away immediately.

—*adapted from* Every Young Man's Battle

FIX YOUR EYES ON THE STRAIGHT AND NARROW

Garrett said, "Honestly, I'd never really guarded my eyes before or even thought about it. I watched any movies I wanted, and I looked way too long at the girls at school, but I really didn't think these things affected my life. But after my mom read your book and told me about it, I began to wonder. So I paid more attention to my eyes over the next day or so, and I found that they were collecting more sexual gratification than I'd thought."

—*adapted from* Every Young Man's Battle

I will set before my eyes
    no vile thing.

PSALM 101:3, NIV

Look straight ahead, and fix your eyes on what lies before you. Mark out a straight path for your feet; then stick to the path and stay safe. Don't get sidetracked; keep your feet from following evil.

PROVERBS 4:25-27, NLT

Turn away my eyes from looking at worthless things, And revive me in Your way.

PSALM 119:37, NKJV

I will tell who can live here: All who are honest and fair…who shut their eyes to all enticement to do wrong.

ISAIAH 33:15, TLB

If your right eye causes you to sin, gouge it out and throw it away. It is better for you to lose one part of your body than for your whole body to be thrown into hell.

MATTHEW 5:29, NIV

DON'T UNDERESTIMATE THE POWER OF LUST

If you want freedom from sexual sin, you must put the ax to the roots. What are the roots? That you're stopping short of God's standard, accepting (through your eyes and your mind) more than a hint of immorality in your life.

—*adapted from* **Every Man's Battle**

But put on the Lord Jesus Christ, and make no provision
for the flesh in regard to its lusts.

ROMANS 13:14, NASB

I say then: Walk in the Spirit, and you shall not fulfill
the lust of the flesh. For the flesh lusts against the Spirit,
and the Spirit against the flesh; and these are contrary
to one another, so that you do not do the things that
you wish.

GALATIANS 5:16-17, NKJV

When you follow the desires of your sinful nature, your
lives will produce these evil results: sexual immorality,
impure thoughts, eagerness for lustful pleasure, envy,
drunkenness, wild parties, and other kinds of sin. Let me
tell you again, as I have before, that anyone living that sort
of life will not inherit the Kingdom of God.

GALATIANS 5:19,21, NLT

Beloved, I beg you as sojourners and pilgrims, abstain
from fleshly lusts which war against the soul.

1 PETER 2:11, NKJV

Put on the full armor of God so that you can take your
stand against the devil's schemes. For our struggle is not
against flesh and blood, but against the rulers, against the
authorities, against the powers of this dark world and

against the spiritual forces of evil in the heavenly realms.
Therefore put on the full armor of God, so that when the
day of evil comes, you may be able to stand your ground,
and after you have done everything, to stand. Stand firm
then, with the belt of truth buckled around your waist,
with the breastplate of righteousness in place, and with
your feet fitted with the readiness that comes from the
gospel of peace. In addition to all this, take up the shield of
faith, with which you can extinguish all the flaming arrows
of the evil one. Take the helmet of salvation and the sword
of the Spirit, which is the word of God.

EPHESIANS 6:11-17, NIV

Sheol (the place of the dead) and Abaddon (the place of
destruction) are never satisfied; so [the lust of] the eyes of
man is never satisfied.

PROVERBS 27:20, AMP

CONTINUE TO FIGHT THE GOOD FIGHT

Fight the good fight for what we believe. Hold tightly to
the eternal life that God has given you, which you have
confessed so well before many witnesses.

1 TIMOTHY 6:12, NLT

Cling tightly to your faith in Christ and always keep your
conscience clear, doing what you know is right. For some

people have disobeyed their consciences and have deliberately done what they knew was wrong.

1 TIMOTHY 1:19, TLB

My son, keep my words
    and treasure up my commandments with you;
keep my commandments and live,
    keep my teachings as the apple of your eye;
bind them on your fingers,
    write them on the tablet of your heart.
Say to wisdom, "You are my sister,"
    and call insight your intimate friend;
to preserve you from the loose woman,
    from the adventuress with her smooth words.

PROVERBS 7:1-5, RSV

dodging enemy fire

In transforming your mind, you'll be taking an active, conscious role in capturing rogue thoughts, but in the long run, the mind will wash itself and will begin to work naturally for you and your purity by capturing such thoughts. With the eyes bouncing away from sexual images, and the mind policing itself, your defenses will grow incredibly strong.

—Every Young Man's Battle

GUARD YOUR CONVERSATION

Don't talk dirty or silly. That kind of talk doesn't fit our style.

EPHESIANS 5:4, MSG

The thoughts of the wicked are an abomination
        to the LORD,
But the words of the pure are pleasant.

PROVERBS 15:26, NKJV

Words from a wise man's mouth are gracious,
        but a fool is consumed by his own lips.

ECCLESIASTES 10:12, NIV

If anyone considers himself religious and yet does not keep a tight rein on his tongue, he deceives himself and his religion is worthless.

JAMES 1:26, NIV

And the tongue is a fire, a world of iniquity. The tongue is so set among our members that it defiles the whole body, and sets on fire the course of nature; and it is set on fire by hell.

JAMES 3:6, NKJV

Keep your tongue from evil and your lips from speaking deceit.

PSALM 34:13, AMP

Avoid all perverse talk; stay far from corrupt speech.

PROVERBS 4:24, NLT

It would be shameful even to mention here those pleasures of darkness which the ungodly do.

EPHESIANS 5:12, TLB

The fear of the LORD is to hate evil;
Pride and arrogance and the evil way
And the perverse mouth I hate.

PROVERBS 8:13, NKJV

For he that will love life, and see good days, let him refrain his tongue from evil, and his lips that they speak no guile.

1 PETER 3:10, KJV

EXAMINE HOW YOU SPEND YOUR TIME

There are young women you know who hit every attraction key on your keyboard. Among those may be an old girlfriend to whom you're still deeply attached because of your past sexual sins. Because of your former intimacy, she may seem yours for the taking in your mind. But you must lead her out of your corral and stop lurking at her door.

—*adapted from* Every Young Man's Battle

If my heart has been enticed by a woman,
> or if I have lurked at my neighbor's door,
then may my wife grind another man's grain,
> and may other men sleep with her.
For that would have been shameful,
> a sin to be judged.

JOB 31:9-11, NIV

So teach us to number our days, that we may get us a heart of wisdom.

PSALM 90:12, AMP

So be careful how you live, not as fools but as those who are wise. Make the most of every opportunity for doing good in these evil days.

EPHESIANS 5:15-16, NLT

REMEMBER THAT OTHERS ARE WATCHING

So be careful how you act; these are difficult days.

EPHESIANS 5:15, TLB

Behave yourselves wisely [living prudently and with discretion] in your relations with those of the outside world (the non-Christians), making the very most of the time and seizing (buying up) the opportunity.

COLOSSIANS 4:5, AMP

He must also have a good reputation with outsiders, so that he will not fall into disgrace and into the devil's trap.

1 TIMOTHY 3:7, NIV

Try to live in peace with everyone, and seek to live a clean and holy life.

HEBREWS 12:14, NLT

A good name is to be more desired than great wealth, Favor is better than silver and gold.

PROVERBS 22:1, NASB

A good reputation is more valuable than the most expensive perfume.

ECCLESIASTES 7:1, TLB

PRACTICE THE FINE ART OF DISCRETION

Limit the times you're alone and in a highly excitable situation. Do things with friends of both sexes. Go on group dates. Limit the amount of touching *and* the amount of kissing. Whatever your defenses, set your rules and then be disciplined.

Walk in truth.

—Every Young Man's Battle

Discretion will protect you, and understanding will guard you.

PROVERBS 2:11, NIV

I, wisdom, dwell together with prudence;
I possess knowledge and discretion.

PROVERBS 8:12, NIV

My son…
Keep sound wisdom and discretion,
So they will be life to your soul
And adornment to your neck.

PROVERBS 3:21-22, NASB

Discretion is a life-giving fountain to those who possess it, but discipline is wasted on fools.

PROVERBS 16:22, NLT

A good man deals graciously and lends;
He will guide his affairs with discretion.

PSALM 112:5, NKJV

PURSUE WISDOM AND COMMON SENSE

What are you doing to do when other guys show you pornography? What are you going to do when that cute girl gets you alone and starts unbuttoning her blouse? Whose voices will you hear? Will it be God's voice, or your friend's telling you to go for it? God's voice had better be loud and crystal clear because it will probably be the only one whispering, "Flee immorality, Son."

—*adapted from* Every Man's Battle

My son, if you receive my words
    and treasure up my commandments with you,
making your ear attentive to wisdom
    and inclining your heart to understanding;
yes, if you cry out for insight
    and raise your voice for understanding,
if you seek it like silver
    and search for it as for hidden treasures;
then you will understand the fear of the LORD
    and find the knowledge of God.
For the LORD gives wisdom;
    from his mouth come knowledge and understanding;

he stores up sound wisdom for the upright;
    he is a shield to those who walk in integrity,
guarding the paths of justice
    and preserving the way of his saints.

PROVERBS 2:1-8, RSV

To the man who pleases him, God gives wisdom, knowledge and happiness.

ECCLESIASTES 2:26, NIV

He who trusts in himself is a fool,
    but he who walks in wisdom is kept safe.

PROVERBS 28:26, NIV

Doing wrong is fun for a fool, while wise conduct is a pleasure to the wise.

PROVERBS 10:23, NLT

And the work of righteousness will be peace,
And the service of righteousness, quietness and confidence
    forever.

ISAIAH 32:17, NASB

How blessed is the man who finds wisdom
And the man who gains understanding.
For her profit is better than the profit of silver

And her gain better than fine gold.
She is more precious than jewels;
And nothing you desire compares with her.

PROVERBS 3:13-15, NASB

Acquire wisdom! Acquire understanding!
Do not forget nor turn away from the words of my
          mouth.
Do not forsake her [wisdom], and she will guard you;
Love her, and she will watch over you.
The beginning of wisdom is: Acquire wisdom;
And with all your acquiring, get understanding.

PROVERBS 4:5-7, NASB

Wisdom makes one wise man more powerful
      than ten rulers in a city.

ECCLESIASTES 7:19, NIV

Wisdom brightens a man's face
      and changes its hard appearance.

ECCLESIASTES 8:1, NIV

So I decided to compare wisdom and folly, and anyone
else would come to the same conclusions I [King Solo-
mon] did. Wisdom is of more value than foolishness, just
as light is better than darkness. For the wise person sees,

while the fool is blind. Yet I saw that wise and foolish people share the same fate. Both of them die. Just as the fool will die, so will I. So of what value is all my wisdom? Then I said to myself, "This is all so meaningless!" For the wise person and the fool both die, and in the days to come, both will be forgotten.

ECCLESIASTES 2:12-16, NLT

Wisdom or money can get you almost anything, but it's important to know that only wisdom can save your life.

ECCLESIASTES 7:12, NLT

Buy truth, and do not sell it;
    buy wisdom, instruction, and understanding.

PROVERBS 23:23, RSV

The godly give good advice, but fools are destroyed by their lack of common sense.

PROVERBS 10:21, NLT

The mind of the prudent acquires knowledge,
And the ear of the wise seeks knowledge.

PROVERBS 18:15, NASB

Being wise is as good as being rich; in fact, it is better.

ECCLESIASTES 7:11, NLT

It is better to be criticized by a wise person than to be
  praised by a fool!
Indeed, a fool's laughter is quickly gone, like thorns crack-
  ling in a fire.

ECCLESIASTES 7:5-6, NLT

The discerning heart seeks knowledge,
  but the mouth of a fool feeds on folly.

PROVERBS 15:14, NIV

A house is built by wisdom and becomes strong through
good sense.

PROVERBS 24:3, NLT

the glory of a well-fought battle

GOD WILL REWARD YOUR EFFORTS

All these blessings will come upon you and overtake you if you obey the LORD your God:… The LORD will command the blessing upon you in your barns and in all that you put your hand to, and He will bless you in the land which the LORD your God gives you.

DEUTERONOMY 28:2,8, NASB

The integrity of the upright guides them,
    but the unfaithful are destroyed by their duplicity.

PROVERBS 11:3, NIV

But he who listens to me shall live securely
And will be at ease from the dread of evil.

PROVERBS 1:33, NASB

So you shall keep His statutes and His commandments which I am giving you today, that it may go well with you and with your children after you, and that you may live long on the land which the LORD your God is giving you for all time.

DEUTERONOMY 4:40, NASB

Say to the righteous that it will go well with them,
For they will eat the fruit of their actions.

ISAIAH 3:10, NASB

YOU'LL HAVE PEACE IN YOUR HEART

You will keep in perfect peace all who trust in you,
    whose thoughts are fixed on you!

ISAIAH 26:3, NLT

And the peace of God, which surpasses all comprehension,
will guard your hearts and your minds in Christ Jesus.

PHILIPPIANS 4:7, NASB

I am leaving you with a gift—peace of mind and heart.
And the peace I give isn't like the peace the world gives. So
don't be troubled or afraid.

JOHN 14:27, NLT

Keep putting into practice all you learned from me and
heard from me and saw me doing, and the God of peace
will be with you.

PHILIPPIANS 4:9, NLT

And let the peace that comes from Christ rule in your
hearts. For as members of one body you are all called to
live in peace. And always be thankful.

COLOSSIANS 3:15, NLT

LORD, You will establish peace for us.

ISAIAH 26:12, NASB

THE VICTORY IS WORTH THE STRUGGLE

Therefore, since we are surrounded by so great a cloud of witnesses, let us also lay aside every weight, and sin which clings so closely, and let us run with perseverance the race that is set before us, looking to Jesus the pioneer and perfecter of our faith, who for the joy that was set before him endured the cross, despising the shame, and is seated at the right hand of the throne of God.

Consider him who endured from sinners such hostility against himself, so that you may not grow weary or faint-hearted.

HEBREWS 12:1-3, RSV

And not only this, but we also exult in our tribulations, knowing that tribulation brings about perseverance; and perseverance, proven character; and proven character, hope.

ROMANS 5:3-4, NASB

So when you make a promise to God, don't delay in following through, for God takes no pleasure in fools. Keep all the promises you make to him. It is better to say nothing than to promise something that you don't follow through on. In such cases, your mouth is making you sin. And don't defend yourself by telling the Temple messenger that the promise you made was a mistake. That would make God angry, and he might wipe out everything you have achieved.

Dreaming all the time instead of working is foolishness. And there is ruin in a flood of empty words. Fear God instead.

ECCLESIASTES 5:4-7, NLT

You have persevered and have endured hardships for my name, and have not grown weary.

REVELATION 2:3, NIV

Be assured and understand that the trial and proving of your faith bring out endurance and steadfastness and patience.

JAMES 1:3, AMP

For by these He has granted to us His precious and magnificent promises, so that by them you may become partakers of the divine nature, having escaped the corruption that is in the world by lust. Now for this very reason also, applying all diligence, in your faith supply moral excellence, and in your moral excellence, knowledge, and in your knowledge, self-control, and in your self-control, perseverance, and in your perseverance, godliness, and in your godliness, brotherly kindness, and in your brotherly kindness, love. For if these qualities are yours and are increasing, they render you neither useless nor unfruitful in the true knowledge of our Lord Jesus Christ.

2 PETER 1:4-8, NASB

The night is almost gone, and the day is near. Therefore let us lay aside the deeds of darkness and put on the armor of light.

ROMANS 13:12, NASB

Pay close attention to yourself and to your teaching; persevere in these things, for as you do this you will ensure salvation both for yourself and for those who hear you.

1 TIMOTHY 4:16, NASB

You need to persevere so that when you have done the will of God, you will receive what he has promised.

HEBREWS 10:36, NIV

As it is written:
"No eye has seen,
   no ear has heard,
no mind has conceived
   what God has prepared for those who love him."

1 CORINTHIANS 2:9, NIV

As you know, we consider blessed those who have persevered. You have heard of Job's perseverance and have seen what the Lord finally brought about. The Lord is full of compassion and mercy.

JAMES 5:11, NIV

the ultimate secret
to overcoming sin

The key to victory in the battle for sexual purity lies in the fact that, as believers, we have the Holy Spirit constantly at our side to help us fight our battles. Without His presence, we have little hope of overcoming the pressures of the world. Now is the perfect time to examine your heart and be sure that you have truly entrusted your heart and life to God, guaranteeing for yourself a Companion who will fight with you and for you.

In Scripture, the "Roman Road" teaches us that everyone has sinned (Romans 3:23), the penalty for our sin is death (Romans 6:23), Jesus Christ died for our sins (Romans 5:8), and to be forgiven for our sins, we must believe and confess that Jesus is Lord, because salvation comes only through Jesus Christ (Romans 10:8-10).

Have you walked the truths of the Roman Road? If not, you can come to know Christ right now by reading and confessing this set of verses. When you trust in Christ, you will spend eternity with Him.

THE ROMAN ROAD

Salvation that comes from trusting Christ—which is the message we preach—is already within easy reach. In fact, the Scriptures say, "The message is close at hand; it is on your lips and in your heart."

For if you confess with your mouth that Jesus is Lord and believe in your heart that God raised him from the dead, you will be saved. For it is by believing in your heart that you are made right with God, and it is by confessing with your mouth that you are saved.

ROMANS 10:8-10, NLT

For all have sinned; all fall short of God's glorious standard.

ROMANS 3:23, NLT

For the wages of sin is death, but the free gift of God is eternal life through Christ Jesus our Lord.

ROMANS 6:23, NLT

But God showed his great love for us by sending Christ to die for us while we were still sinners.

ROMANS 5:8, NLT

THE PROMISE OF THE HOLY SPIRIT

But it isn't the new life ahead of you that should transform you. It should be the new life in you.

—*adapted from* Every Young Man's Battle

And I will put my Spirit in you and move you to follow my decrees and be careful to keep my laws.

EZEKIEL 36:27, NIV

But you are not like that. You are controlled by your new nature if you have the Spirit of God living in you. (And remember that if anyone doesn't have the Spirit of Christ living in him, he is not a Christian at all.)

ROMANS 8:9, TLB

For his Holy Spirit speaks to us deep in our hearts and tells us that we are God's children.

ROMANS 8:16, NLT

Those who obey God's commandments live in fellowship with him, and he with them. And we know he lives in us because the Holy Spirit lives in us.

1 JOHN 3:24, NLT

We know that we live in him and he in us, because he has given us of his Spirit.

1 JOHN 4:13, NIV

For as many as are led by the Spirit of God, these are sons of God.

ROMANS 8:14, NKJV

ready your weapons, raise your shield

You're called to lead spiritually, and if you do, you'll go through life without regrets. That's a great place to start as you begin to live on your own, marry, and have a family.

—**Every Young Man's Battle**

A TIME TO CHOOSE

Today I have given you the choice between life and death, between blessings and curses. I call on heaven and earth to witness the choice you make. Oh, that you would choose life, that you and your descendants might live!

DEUTERONOMY 30:19, NLT

Nevertheless, God's solid foundation stands firm, sealed with this inscription: "The Lord knows those who are his," and, "Everyone who confesses the name of the Lord must turn away from wickedness."

2 TIMOTHY 2:19, NIV

There is a time for everything,
a season for every activity under heaven.
A time to be born and a time to die.
A time to plant and a time to harvest.
A time to kill and a time to heal.
A time to tear down and a time to rebuild.
A time to cry and a time to laugh.
A time to grieve and a time to dance.

A time to scatter stones and a time to gather stones.

A time to embrace and a time to turn away.

A time to search and a time to lose.

A time to keep and a time to throw away.

A time to tear and a time to mend.

A time to be quiet and a time to speak up.

A time to love and a time to hate.

A time for war and a time for peace.

ECCLESIASTES 3:1-8, NLT

STEP FORWARD IN THE CONFIDENCE OF GOD'S PROTECTION

Fight the good fight of the faith. Take hold of the eternal life to which you were called when you made your good confession in the presence of many witnesses.

1 TIMOTHY 6:12, NIV

Put on God's whole armor [the armor of a heavy-armed soldier which God supplies], that you may be able success-fully to stand up against [all] the strategies and the deceits of the devil.

EPHESIANS 6:11, AMP

But let us who live in the light keep sober, protected by the armor of faith and love, and wearing as our helmet the happy hope of salvation.

1 THESSALONIANS 5:8, TLB

He will cover you with His pinions,
And under His wings you may seek refuge;
His faithfulness is a shield and bulwark.

PSALM 91:4, NASB

For surely, O LORD, you bless the righteous;
you surround them with your favor as with a shield.

PSALM 5:12, NIV

We depend on the LORD alone to save us.
Only he can help us, protecting us like a shield.

PSALM 33:20, NLT

For Jehovah God is our Light and our Protector. He gives us grace and glory. No good thing will he withhold from those who walk along his paths.

PSALM 84:11, TLB

a final word

But remember this: It's not the act of defining sexual boundaries that makes you a spiritual leader—it's the act of defending them.

> One final word, friends. We ask you—urge is more like it—that you keep on doing what we told you to do to please God, not in a dogged religious plod, but in a living, spirited dance. You know the guidelines we laid out for you from the Master Jesus. God wants you to live a pure life.
>
> Keep yourselves from sexual promiscuity.
>
> Learn to appreciate and give dignity to your body, not abusing it, as is so common among those who know nothing of God.
>
> **1 THESSALONIANS 4:1-3,** MSG

Steve can be reached by e-mail at sarterburn@newlife.com.

Fred can be reached by e-mail at fred@stoekergroup.com.

every man's battle
workshops

from New Life Ministries

New Life Ministries receives hundreds of calls every month from Christian men who are struggling to stay pure in the midst of daily challenges to their sexual integrity and from pastors who are looking for guidance in how to keep fragile marriages from falling apart all around them.

As part of our commitment to equip individuals to win these battles, New Life Ministries has developed biblically based workshops directly geared to answer these needs. These workshops are held several times per year around the country.

- Our workshops **for men** are structured to equip men with the tools necessary to maintain sexual integrity and enjoy healthy, productive relationships.

- Our workshops **for church leaders** are targeted to help pastors and men's ministry leaders develop programs to help families being attacked by this destructive addiction.

Some comments from previous workshop attendees:

"An awesome, life-changing experience. Awesome teaching, teacher, content and program."   —DAVE

"God has truly worked a great work in me since the EMB workshop. I am fully confident that with God's help, I will be restored in my ministry position. Thank you for your concern. I realize that this is a battle, but I now have the weapons of warfare as mentioned in Ephesians 6:10, and I am using them to gain victory!"   —KEN

"It's great to have a workshop you can confidently recommend to anyone without hesitation, knowing that it is truly life changing. Your labors are not in vain!"   —DR. BRAD STENBERG, Pasadena, CA

If sexual temptation is threatening your marriage or your church, please call
1-800-NEW-LIFE to speak with one of our specialists.

To learn more about WaterBrook Press and view
our catalog of products, log on to our Web site:
www.waterbrookpress.com